insight text guide

Anja Drummond

In Cold Blood

Truman Capote

First published in 2017, reprinted in 2019, 2020, 2021, 2023.

Insight Publications Pty Ltd
3/350 Charman Road
Cheltenham VIC 3192
Australia
Tel: +61 3 8571 4950
Fax: +61 3 8571 0257
Email: books@insightpublications.com.au

www.insightpublications.com.au

A catalogue record for this book is available from the National Library of Australia

Truman Capote's In Cold Blood / Anja Drummond

ISBNs:
9781925485790 (print)
9781925485806 (digital)
9781925485813 (bundle: print + digital)

Cover design: Gisela Beer, based on a concept by The Modern Art Production Group

Printed in Australia by Ligare

contents

CHARACTER MAP

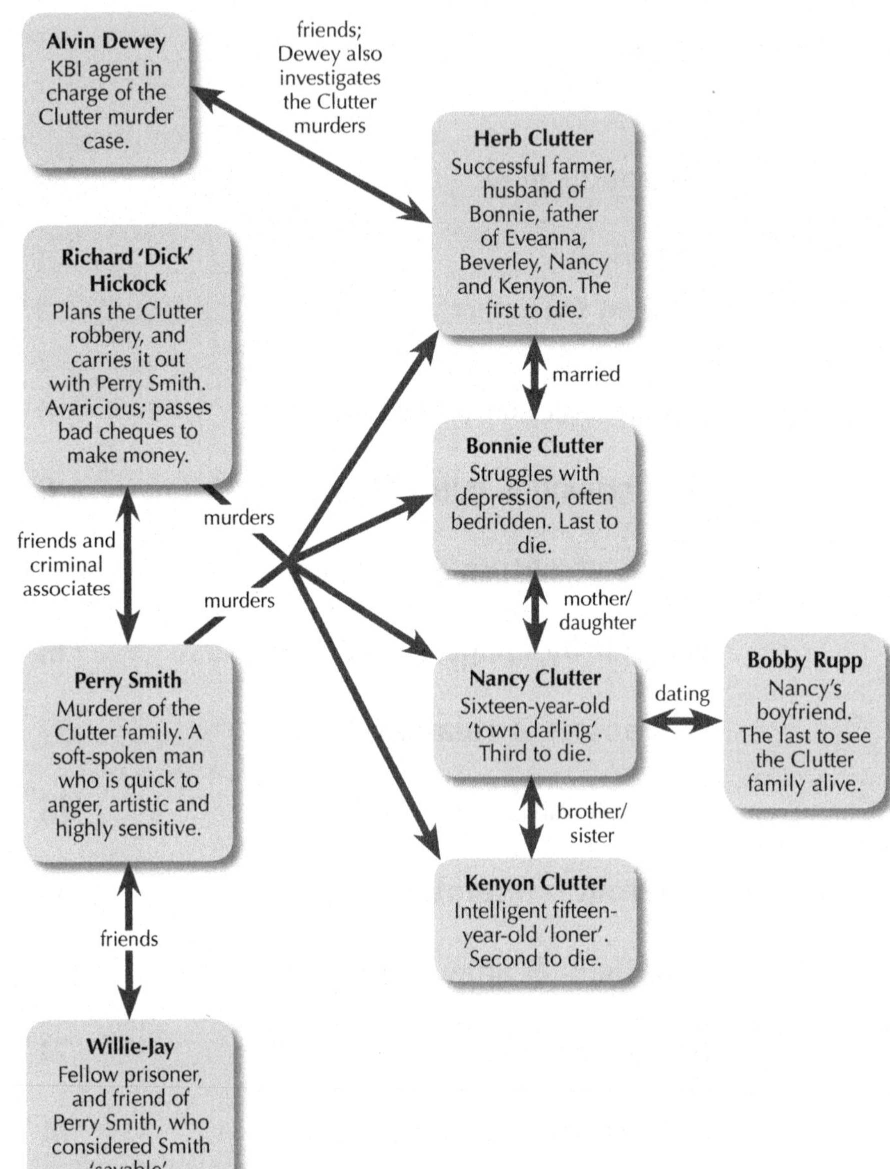

OVERVIEW

About the author

The only child of a failed marriage between Lillie Mae Faulk and Arch Persons, Truman Capote was born Truman Streckfus Persons on 30 September 1924 in New Orleans, Louisiana. Truman's early childhood was marked by neglect on the part of his parents. This negligence included locking Truman in their hotel room when they travelled and instructing staff not to let him out even if he screamed (which he often did). When not under his parents' care, Truman was sent to live with his relations in Monroeville, Alabama, where he became friends with Nelle Harper Lee (author of *To Kill a Mockingbird*). Capote and Lee's friendship proved to be lifelong; the foundation of it was a bond of 'common anguish' caused by 'the bruises of parental rejection' that had left both of them 'shattered by loneliness' (Clarke 1988).

In 1931, Lillie Mae left her husband and moved to New York, where she changed her name to Nina, divorced Arch, and married a wealthy Cuban immigrant named Joe Capote. Truman moved in with his mother and stepfather in 1933 and was officially adopted by Capote in 1935, at which time Truman's name was changed to Truman Garcia Capote. Capote's relationship with his mother continued to be difficult. As she descended into alcoholism she often abused Truman because of his effeminate nature and his homosexuality. At school, Capote was considered a mediocre student, though his talent for writing was apparent from an early age. He attended a private boys' school in Manhattan from 1933 to 1936, after which Nina sent him to a military academy until 1937, in an effort to make him more masculine. At both schools, the petite and effeminate Capote was the target of sexual advances, including, according to biographer Gerald Clarke (1988), a 'sorry initiation into the mysteries of sex' when he was sexually abused by a teacher in the sixth grade. As he got older, Truman and his mother were mostly estranged from each other. Nina committed suicide in 1954.

Capote had no formal education beyond high school. Instead, at age seventeen he found clerical work at *The New Yorker*, the magazine that would later publish *In Cold Blood* in serial form. There he continued to develop his eccentric and flamboyant behaviour and dress, and was increasingly open about his homosexuality. After publishing several short stories, Capote published his first novel, *Other Voices, Other Rooms*, in 1948 at the age of twenty-four. This autobiographical coming-of-age novel was widely acclaimed, and many successful books followed, including *The Grass Harp* (1951) and *Breakfast at Tiffany's* (1958). Capote became a friend and confidant of many well-known people, and had a long-term relationship with American novelist and playwright Jack Dunphy, with whom he lived in Europe for much of the 1950s.

Capote returned to the United States in the late 1950s hoping to compose what he termed a 'nonfiction novel'. On the morning of Monday 16 November 1959, Capote opened *The New York Times* and found at the back of the paper a one-column story headlined, 'WEALTHY FARMER, 3 OF FAMILY SLAIN', which began: 'A wealthy wheat farmer, his wife and their two young children were found shot to death today in their home. They had been killed by shotgun blasts at close range after being bound and gagged.' Capote set out to investigate further, and spent the next six years researching the Clutter killings and following the fates of the murderers, Richard Hickock and Perry Smith.

Published in January 1966, *In Cold Blood* was a critical and commercial success. However, Capote's work took an emotional toll on him – he claimed that writing the book 'scraped me right down to the marrow of my bones' and 'nearly killed me' (Wood 1988). The emotional trauma of writing the book was difficult to overcome and Capote became increasingly dependent on drugs and alcohol. While he continued to publish, his subsequent works never achieved the same critical acclaim as *In Cold Blood*. Capote died on 25 August 1984.

Synopsis

Part 1: The Last to See Them Alive

The text opens in the town of Holcomb, a small and isolated rural settlement in western Kansas that 'few Americans – in fact, few Kansans –

had ever heard of' (p.16). The quiet of the town is broken on 15 November 1959 by 'four shotgun blasts that, all told, ended six human lives' (p.17); the victims of these four blasts are the Clutter family. Herb, Bonnie, Nancy and Kenyon Clutter are prominent and respected members of the community, and their successes are, for the most part, emblematic of the achievement of the American dream. Part 1 retraces the steps of each member of the family on what was to be the final day of their lives, outlining their activities and giving an insight into their personalities through the recollections of the last people to see them alive.

Alternating with the account of the family's day are descriptions of the perpetrators of the murders – Richard Hickock (known as Dick) and Perry Smith. Paroled from prison, Dick and Perry prepare for 'the Perfect score' (pp.55–6), believing that Herb Clutter keeps a large sum of cash in a safe. The preparations of the pair seem shambolic, but their intent is made clear – they are prepared for murder and Dick, in particular, emphasises that no one will be left alive. As the activities of the Clutter household draw to a close, the killers come nearer, pulling in to the Clutter driveway in the early hours of the morning. The details of the murders are withheld at this point, but it is clear that the murderers do not find any cash at the Clutter household, yet kill the family anyway. The killers pass a series of bad cheques before they flee to Mexico, while the people of Holcomb learn of the murders.

Part 2: Persons Unknown

The Kansas Bureau of Investigation (KBI) is put on the case. A team of investigators, led by Alvin Dewey, tries to piece together what has happened, but is confused as to the motive of the crime and hindered by a lack of evidence. The only clues to the identities of the killer or killers are two footprints. The only suspect, Nancy's boyfriend Bobby Rupp, is cleared by a lie-detector test, and the residents of Holcomb struggle to cope with the lack of answers regarding the crime. The residents become suspicious of each other, lock their doors, and gossip incessantly as they wonder about the truth of what happened, and why.

Meanwhile, Dick and Perry go broke in Mexico and decide to return to the United States. As Perry packs his belongings for the trip, he reflects on his various possessions and their meaning to his life. Among the possessions he packs are two pairs of boots.

Part 3: Answer

When Dick's former cellmate, Floyd Wells, reveals to authorities that Dick had told him of his plan to rob and kill the Clutters, the KBI launches a manhunt for Dick and Perry. The pair return to Kansas City, where they pass more bad cheques and narrowly escape a brush with authorities before heading to Miami for Christmas. Again running out of money, they head west once more, making their way to Las Vegas. Perry is collecting some of the belongings he packed in Mexico, including the boots, when he and Dick are arrested. The detectives' careful handling of the interrogation of the two men pays off, with first Dick then Perry making detailed confessions. Dick claims that Perry perpetrated all four murders, while Perry claims Dick is responsible for the murders of the women. The murderers are escorted to Garden City where their trial will be held.

Part 4: The Corner

Dick and Perry are put on trial and found guilty of four counts of murder. In accordance with Kansas law, they are sentenced to death by hanging. Over the course of five years, the killers' 'ride on the Big Swing' (p.336) is delayed by a series of appeals. The appeals are ultimately unsuccessful and both are hanged on 14 April 1965. At the execution, Perry apologises for his actions while Dick states that he has no hard feelings against the state. Alvin Dewey is present at the hanging but does not feel relieved.

Character summaries

Herb Clutter

The forty-eight-year-old father of four is a self-made man who, through hard work and perseverance, has achieved moderate success. Herb Clutter is a devout Methodist and heavily involved in his community. A strict but loving father, Herb takes on many of the household and parenting duties when his wife is unwell. He is the first member of the family to be killed.

Bonnie Clutter

Bonnie is forty-five years old when she dies and is the final member of the Clutter family to be killed. After developing postnatal depression following the birth of her first child, Bonnie suffered from recurrent bouts of depression that necessitated several hospitalisations.

Nancy Clutter

The third victim, sixteen-year-old Nancy is considered the 'town darling' (p.18). Like her father, Nancy is good-natured and heavily involved in her community, showing leadership and generosity. Nancy is dating Bobby Rupp at the time of her death.

Kenyon Clutter

The second victim, fifteen-year-old Kenyon, is a quiet, intelligent young man but is considered a loner with few friends.

Alvin Dewey

Dewey is the lead investigator for the KBI on the Clutter case and the 'hero' of Capote's narrative. He is close friends with Herb Clutter. His obsession with solving the case is detrimental to his health. Much of the narrative is told from his perspective.

Richard Eugene 'Dick' Hickock

The mastermind of the Clutter murders, Dick grew up in a poor but loving family. A car accident in which he suffered severe head injuries also left his face disfigured. Married several times, he is motivated by lust and greed, and has paedophilic tendencies. He makes money through such crimes as passing bad cheques.

Perry Edward Smith

Hickock's co-conspirator in the murder of the Clutter family, Perry is a short man with a large torso and small legs. He had a difficult childhood in which he was abandoned and abused. A motorcycle accident that severely damaged his legs leaves him in constant pain. Perry is soft-spoken, quick to anger, artistic and sensitive.

NOTE: The number of characters in *In Cold Blood* precludes listing all of them. The following are the most important minor characters.

Lowell Lee Andrews

Murderer on death row who killed his parents and sister. Diagnosed schizophrenic.

Mrs Hideo Ashida

Resident of Holcomb and member of the 4-H Club.

Special Agent Roy Church

One of the lead detectives on the Clutter case.

Mrs Myrtle Clare

Postmistress of Holcomb post office. Daughter of Sadie Truit.

Don Cullivan

Religious friend of Perry's from the army. Provides friendship to Perry following his arrest. Seeks to guide Perry to salvation.

Special Agent Clarence Duntz

One of the lead detectives on the Clutter case.

Beverly English (nee Clutter)

The second daughter Herb and Bonnie Clutter. Out of town when the murder is committed. Marries Vere English in the same week as the funeral for her family.

Nancy Ewalt

Close friend of Nancy Clutter. First to discover Nancy's body (with Susan Kidwell).

Arthur Fleming

Attorney appointed to defend Perry.

Logan Green

Prosecuting attorney in the Clutter trial.

Paul Helm

Caretaker of River Valley Farm. His wife is the housekeeper for the Clutter family.

Walter and Eunice Hickock

Dick's father and mother. Walter is dying of cancer.

Susan Kidwell

Nancy Clutter's best friend. Discovers Nancy's body (with Nancy Ewalt).

Josephine Meier

Wife of Wendle Meier (the Undersheriff of Finney County). She shows kindness to Perry while is he kept in the women's cell in the courthouse. Her insights into Perry's nature are important.

Special Agent Harold Nye

One of the lead detectives on the Clutter case.

Bobby Rupp

Nancy's boyfriend and 'a school basketball hero' (p.20). Initially a suspect in the Clutter case and the last person to see the Clutter family alive (other than the killers).

'Tex' John Smith and Julie 'Flo' Buckskin

Perry's father and mother.

Floyd Wells

Inmate at Lansing Prison and former employee of Herb Clutter. Wells tells Dick about the Clutter farm and wrongly states that Herb has a safe filled with cash. Wells' information is crucial to the case being solved.

Willie-Jay

Fellow prisoner and friend of Perry. Perry considers Willie-Jay to be his 'real and only friend' (p.53).

BACKGROUND & CONTEXT

Because he was writing about events that were occurring at the time, the author's context and the context of the text are similar. However, it is important to understand that the society in which Capote mixed in New York was markedly different to that of the Clutters in Kansas.

Prosperity and fear in 1950s America

Dwight D Eisenhower was the thirty-fourth President of the United States of America, serving from 1953 until 1961. His presidency saw a continuation of the American economic boom that followed World War II. The growth in jobs, product availability, public investment and so on led to changing social patterns and structures, including increased urbanisation, improved standards of living and the emergence of consumerism. In United States heartlands such as Holcomb, Kansas, citizens felt confident and secure, trusting in the notion of the American dream. Importantly, not all American citizens benefited during this era, with aspects of identity such as race and class making it more difficult for some Americans to realise the dream.

Key point

The 'American dream' refers to the idea that any American can become successful through hard work and perseverance. Success in terms of the dream is generally understood as attaining a good job, a nice house, a family and plenty of money.

Despite the increased affluence of the United States in the 1950s and 1960s, this was also a period of national anxiety. There were genuine fears of communism, and widespread paranoia led to investigations of many Americans suspected of communist leanings (in particular, artists and homosexuals). Literary and artistic radicalism was largely inhibited during this period. Instead there was an emphasis on cultural conformity and, as a consequence of the anti-communist efforts of such public figures as Senator Joseph McCarthy, books such as JD Salinger's *The Catcher in the Rye* and Ray Bradbury's *Fahrenheit 451* were banned. Literature was frequently judged on its moral qualities.

However, by the late 1950s, distinct countercultures and youth cultures (such as that associated with rock-and-roll music) were starting to emerge in the United States, as were new political movements such as civil rights and feminism. University students began to question the rampant materialism and conservatism of their society and many artists challenged the ideas that had hitherto dominated the era.

Capote's sexuality

At a time when homosexuality was viewed by mainstream society as a sickness and as a deviation from the norm, Truman Capote was very open about being gay. Among the left-wing progressive society of New York, this was not an issue, but when Capote arrived in Holcomb he was 'greeted with derision' and perceived as 'someone coming off the moon' (Clarke 1988). To overcome the obstacles created by his difference, Capote was initially reliant upon his close friend Nelle Harper Lee (author of *To Kill a Mockingbird*), who was able to inveigle her way into the homes and hearts of the people of Holcomb and persuade them to accept Capote and grant him interviews.

The Clutter murders

On Sunday 15 November 1959, Finney County Sheriff Earl Robinson and Undersheriff Wendle Meier were called to River Valley Farm in Holcomb after family friends discovered the body of Nancy Clutter. After locating Nancy's body, the men searched the house and discovered the bodies of Herb, Bonnie and Kenyon. The murders were brutal and apparently without motive. They were described by Logan Sanford, director of the KBI, as 'the goriest crime I have ever seen in Kansas' (*Garden City Telegram* 1959).

GENRE, STRUCTURE & LANGUAGE

Genre

New Journalism was an American literary movement in the 1960s and '70s that sought to combine journalistic research with literary elements in the reporting of stories about real-life events. Truman Capote is recognised as one of the originators of this movement. These writers relied upon traditional methods of investigative reporting, gathering information through research, interviews and observations. But rather than producing their findings in the form of feature stories for newspapers, they fashioned them into extended narratives with well-developed characters, sustained dialogue, the graphic rendering of events, and strong plots marked by dramatic tension. Thus, they were able to 'dramatise and give psychological order to a piece of implacably authentic, documented life' (Steiner 1965).

Structure

In Cold Blood takes the form of a novel, featuring characters, a distinctive narrative voice and a story structure that includes an introduction, rising action, climax and resolution. Capote arranged the events surrounding the murder of the Clutter family and the capture and eventual execution of the murderers in order to reveal causal relationships between key moments that impacted on the fates of the characters. Although the narrative is mostly linear, part of Capote's skilful plotting is the withholding of the account of the murders until the end of Part 3, in which Perry confesses, thus generating interest and suspense.

Capote employs the principle of relevance that dictates the structure of a news report. In a news report, the main points of the story are given at the beginning; Capote similarly gives the most important information first and only then begins to gradually unfold the details. However, Capote has clearly shaped *In Cold Blood* as a storyteller rather than as a reporter.

Interweaving of narrative threads

Alternating between the stories (narrative threads) involving different key characters in the text allows Capote to use each thread to cast light on the other while holding back key information or delaying plot development. When these narrative threads intersect, key revelations and events, such as the details of the murders of the Clutter family and the arrests of the murderers, are played out.

Foreshadowing

Capote's use of foreshadowing enables the reader to anticipate events that occur later in the narrative. The use of this technique reminds us that the narrative is constructed, and not a straightforward documentary record of events.

Language

Narrative viewpoint

The events and observations of *In Cold Blood* are primarily conveyed through an omniscient third-person narrator who might be understood to generally represent the author's own views. However, Capote is careful to present an appearance of objectivity and avoids placing himself within the narrative or sharing his personal connection to the case. This veneer of objectivity needs to be carefully scrutinised. In an interview, Capote stated:

> I make my own comment by what I choose to tell and how I choose to tell it. It is true that an author is more in control of fictional characters because he can do anything he wants with them as long as they stay credible. But in the non-fiction novel one can also manipulate: If I put something in which I don't agree about I can always set it in a context of qualification without having to step into the story myself to set the reader straight. (Plimpton 1966)

The reader should be alert to Capote's motives and personal feelings throughout the text, and consider how his presentation of evidence reveals his own views and values. In particular, it should be noted that while Capote maintains the third-person viewpoint, at times he gives the narrative voice to the murderers. This technique invites the reader to form a bond with the killers, whose daily activities reveal their ordinariness, as well as their broken natures.

Tone and style

Capote's narrative style tends to be ornate and his tone serious. Informal language and colloquial expressions are used in the parts of the text presented from the point of view of others, and in dialogue, thus creating a strong sense of social context, time and place. The variations in language style reveal much about the different characters. For example, Tex John Smith's letter to Perry is transcribed as it was written, with spelling and grammatical errors that indicate his lack of education.

The lyricism of much of Capote's writing is created, in part, through the use of poetic techniques such as assonance, alliteration, sibilance and personification. These techniques are used to influence the mood of a scene and enhance characterisation.

Imagery

Capote uses imagery to aid his descriptions, but he also uses it thematically. The wind that blows voices over fields is an example. At the end of *In Cold Blood,* Capote provides a scene that is entirely fictional – Alvin Dewey meets Susan Kidwell by chance at the Clutter graves. As she leaves:

> [S]he disappeared down the path, a pretty girl in a hurry, her smooth hair swinging, shining – just such a young woman as Nancy might have been. Then, starting home, he walked towards the trees, and under them, leaving behind him the big sky, the whisper of wind voices in the wind-bent wheat. (p.343)

Symbolism

Symbols are employed throughout the text, most often in association with Perry Smith. For example:

- Perry has a dream of a large yellow bird, 'taller than Jesus' (p.101), which rescues him from his abusers. This avenging angel is biblically allegorical and also alludes to maternal and vigilante themes.
- The sound of coyotes is often heard around Holcomb; when being extradited back to Kansas, Perry contemplates 'the carcasses of shotgunned coyotes festooning ranch fences' (p.234). Much like the locals hang the carcasses to scare away other coyotes and keep the livestock safe, Dick and Perry are hanged as a deterrent to other criminals.
- Two grey tomcats scavenge as a means of survival, prowling for birds and other roadkill stuck to the grilles of vehicles in Garden City. Observing these cats from his prison cell, Perry says 'most of my life I've done what they're doing' (p.265) and is unable to watch them further.

Irony

In Cold Blood contains numerous example of dramatic irony. For example, there is a poignant irony in Nancy's laying out, in her final hours, her clothes for church, including the 'red velveteen dress' that will become the 'dress in which she was to be buried' (p.67). There is also irony in the fact that Dick and Perry entered the home of the Clutters expecting to find a safe filled with at least $10 000 but instead left with only 'between forty and fifty dollars' (p.248). Mrs Ashida's comment to Herb – 'I can't imagine you afraid. No matter what happened, you'd talk your way out of it' (p.47) – is also ironic in view of his ultimate fate.

Verisimilitude

Verisimilitude refers to something being given the appearance of being true or real. Capote creates verisimilitude in the portraits of the town of Holcomb, the Clutter family, the criminals and so on, through a range of techniques. He includes details such as what Herb Clutter eats for breakfast and Perry Smith's aspirin-chewing, incorporating documentary material into a narrative form. This documentary-style realism is enhanced by Capote's often poetic and lyrical language, as well as by his incorporation of dialogue recreated following extensive interviews with those who were present at different moments. Interestingly, when the syndicated version of *In Cold Blood* was published in *The New Yorker* magazine (1965), the Editor's Note at the top of the first instalment read: 'All quotations in this article are taken either from official records or from conversations, transcribed verbatim, between the author and the principals'.

CHAPTER-BY CHAPTER ANALYSIS

Part 1: The Last to See Them Alive (pp.15–68)

Summary: *Saturday, 14 November, 1959. Herb, Bonnie, Nancy and Kenyon Clutter go about their daily activities, while Perry Smith and Dick Hickock prepare for 'the Perfect score'. As the day ends, the killers draw closer to Holcomb.*

From the opening lines, Capote's impressionistic style and rich language evoke a sense of people and place. Holcomb is depicted as a 'lonesome' and isolated place, untouched by the rapidly changing outside world, with streets 'unnamed, unshaded, unpaved' (p.15). The inhabitants of Holcomb are 'in general, a prosperous people' (p.16) whose lives are marked by faith in God and in the American dream. These people are 'quite content to exist inside ordinary life' in a place where 'drama, in the shape of exceptional happenings' (p.17) does not occur. In spite of his claims of objectivity, Capote's personal views are gently woven into his commentary. This image of conservative middle America is reinforced by Capote's later descriptions of Garden City. This setting is intruded upon by 'four shotgun blasts that, all told, ended six human lives' (p.17). These blasts disrupt the somnolent nature of Holcomb while simultaneously engaging the reader's interest and foregrounding several of Capote's key themes. From here, Capote employs a dual sequential narrative structure, weaving together the stories of two seemingly disparate sets of characters: the Clutters and the killers.

Capote reconstructs the movements and conversations of the day based on the testimonies of the locals who were 'the last to see them alive'. The Clutters have firm roots in the community and appear to epitomise the American dream come true. Herb Clutter 'cut a man's-man figure' (p.17) and has 'in large measure obtained' (p.18) what he wants. His name is 'everywhere respectfully recognized' (p.18). On the last day of his life, Herb reflects on his achievements with pride, then fulfils one of his many obligations as 'a die-hard community booster' (p.33) by 'acting as chairman of the Finney County 4-H Club' (p.46). (The 4-H Club is a community organisation that aims to develop citizenship, responsibility and life skills in young people.) Herb is a strict father – 'his laws were laws' (p.19). Rigid conservatism is evident in Herb's misgivings about Nancy's relationship with Bobby Rupp because 'the Rupp family were Roman Catholics, the Clutters, Methodist – a fact that should in itself be sufficient to terminate whatever fancies she and this boy might have of some day marrying' (p.20). Capote suggests there is tension between generations, as the conservative bonds of American society are tested by the younger generation. Regardless, Herb's children are a source of pride for him. Nancy appears busy, like her father, taking time on her Saturday, among other things, to teach Jolene Katz to make pies.

Though much about the Clutters' lives seems perfect, there are suggestions that appearances can be deceiving. Though active in the community, Kenyon prefers to 'be alone' (p.49), and there is evidence to suggest that he is often fractious with Nancy. In addition, Bonnie Clutter's mental health is a 'serious cause for disquiet' (p.18) for Herb.

The Clutter family's final day contains a number of dark portents of their fate. There is a cruel irony in the fact that Bonnie 'despaired of surviving' the Clutter Thanksgiving get-together or daughter Beverly's wedding because they each necessitate 'making decisions' (p.40), while the revelation that the 'red velveteen dress' which Nancy sets out for church is instead the 'dress in which she was to be buried' (p.67) is imbued with pathos. These and other moments are poignant reminders that the Clutters' lives are about to be extinguished 'in cold blood'.

Key point

Bonnie Clutter's mental state, her tone of 'apology', her 'fear' and her air of being 'defenceless' (p.36) reveal that, rather than mental illness being an issue only for those living on the fringes of society, it exists within the homes of middle America.

The second narrative woven through this section is that of the killers. As he does with the Clutter family, Capote brings his skills as a fiction writer to bear on his nonfiction subjects, cleverly developing his characterisation of the murderers by interweaving their thoughts with descriptions of their physical appearance. Of the two, Perry is handled more sympathetically by Capote. He is revealed to have an interest in the arts and literature, with a particular talent for music. Notably, Perry's meagre 'worldly belongings' (p.26) contrast pathetically with the physical (and emotional) wealth possessed by Herb Clutter.

However, both murderers are distinctly malevolent characters: Dick's face and Perry's body (both damaged in car accidents) hint at a duality within each man's nature. Dick claims to want a 'regular life' in which he has 'a business of his own, a house, a horse to ride, a new car, and "plenty of blonde chicken"' (p.66) but his careful planning of the Clutter robbery contradicts this claim, as does his repeated declaration that they will put 'plenty of hair on them-those walls' (p.49). Meanwhile, Perry's potential split nature is recognised by his friend Willie-Jay, who suggests that Perry, in spite of his sensitivity, suffers from the tragic flaw of '*explosive emotional reaction out of all proportion to the occasion*' (p.54). The killers draw closer to the Clutters throughout the course of the day, until, as Nancy prepares for bed, the reader's anticipation of the imminent event is mirrored in Dick's excited declaration, 'This is it, this is it, this has to be it' (p.68).

Key point

Capote maintains narrative tension throughout this section through the interweaving of the narrative threads, heightening the reader's anticipation of the murder to come. Yet, rather than providing the reader with the release of knowing the precise events of the evening of 15 November, he withholds the details until the end of Part 3.

Key vocabulary

Abstemious: consuming food and drink in moderation.

Beneficence: kindness; charity.

Booster: someone who encourages or 'boosts'.

Coterie: a group of people who associate closely, especially for social reasons.

Genial: cheerful; cordial.

Haranguing: delivering a passionate speech.

Ineffable: inexpressible; unspeakable.

Reticent: not inclined to speak freely; reserved.

Ruminations: musings or ponderings.

Q Identify further examples of Capote's use of irony and foreshadowing in this section. How do these affect the reader's response to the Clutter family killings?

Q What are the similarities and differences between the dreams of the Clutter family and the dreams of Dick and Perry?

Part 1: The Last to See Them Alive (pp.68–84)

Summary: *On Sunday morning, Susan Kidwell and Nancy Ewalt discover the murders. Perry waits in his hotel room, unable to eat; Dick returns home hungry and exhausted. As news of the murders spreads, the town of Holcomb is in fear.*

When Nancy Ewalt and Susan Kidwell discover Nancy's body, their 'screaming' and 'running' (p.70) from the gruesome discovery is like a scene from a Hollywood movie. Their response prepares the reader to be shocked, while Susan's protestation that 'it's only a nosebleed' (p.71) heightens anticipation of the details of the murder while simultaneously suggesting the general disbelief that such a thing could happen. Capote abdicates responsibility for conveying the details, instead inserting an account written by local teacher Larry Hendricks. This documentary-style commentary carries an air of authenticity, and also exculpates Capote from any accusations of being overly graphic. The murder scene is brutal and shocking, the walls 'covered with blood' (p.73). At the same time, elements of the scene seem at odds with the violence of the crimes, such as the chair placed in the bathroom, Nancy's bedcovers 'drawn up to her shoulders' (p.73), and Kenyon's head 'propped by a couple of pillows'. Hendricks also notes the absence of any meaningful evidence other than 'a blood-stained footprint' (p.75).

Hendricks' shock at the murder of 'gentle, kindly people, people *I* knew' (p.76) is echoed by the people of Holcomb. Beginning with Hendricks' recollection of Mrs Kidwell saying, 'Oh Bonnie, Bonnie, what happened? You were so happy, you told me it was all over, you said you'd never be sick again' (p.72), vicious gossip and divisive rumours generate suspicion and fear. Myrtle Clare is quick to suggest that the murders are a consequence of Herb spending 'his whole life in a hurry' and 'running everything, getting jobs maybe other people wanted' (p.79) in his quest to be successful; her theory hints that the Clutters' success is a cause for jealousy among some of the less successful members of the community. The response of most townspeople is 'amazement, shading into dismay; a shallow horror sensation that cold springs of personal fear swiftly deepened' (p.80). This establishes one of Capote's key themes – the loss of the innocence of middle America. Against this scene of a community reeling under the shock of the news, Capote juxtaposes images of the killers, exhausted from their evening's activities. It is difficult for the reader to reconcile the violent images of the slain Clutter family with that of Perry sleeping while his boots soak 'in a washbasin filled with warm, vaguely pink-tinted water' and Dick nonchalantly 'consuming a Sunday dinner' (p.84).

Key point

The public's initial reaction to the crime establishes that their innocence has been shattered, while their gossip indicates a desire for answers, and for evidence that there was some sort of meaningful design behind the murders.

Key vocabulary

Candour: honesty; openness.

Caustic: very critical or sarcastic.

Cortege: a procession.

Q Why does Capote detail the ordinary actions of the killers at the conclusion of this section?

Q Compare the murder of Herb Clutter with that of Nancy. What reasons can you suggest for the differences in the way each is murdered?

Part 2: Persons Unknown (pp.85–130)

Summary: *The KBI, headed by Alvin Dewey, begins its investigation. Perry expresses his worry to Dick that they will be caught. Fear and suspicion spread through Holcomb, and Dick and Perry write a series of hot cheques before fleeing to Mexico.*

A group of Herb Clutter's associates undertakes the gruesome task of cleaning the rooms in which the Clutters were murdered by 'persons unknown'. As they burn some of the 'blood-soiled' (p.86) remnants of the crime scene, Andy Erhart wonders: 'How was it possible that such effort, such plain virtue, could overnight be reduced to this – smoke, thinning as it rose and was received by the big, annihilating sky?' (p.87). The smoke symbolises the fragility of life and the tenuous nature of material wealth, which can be carried away on the wind (a key motif in much of Capote's writing). Erhart's question points to an epistemological crisis that much of the community is experiencing: the world as they know it has been radically altered because 'that family represented everything people hereabouts really value and respect' (p.96). In an attempt to restore people's shattered sense of security, 'locks and bolts are the fastest-going item' (pp.95–6). Furthermore, people are, for the first time, enduring 'the unique experience of distrusting each other' (p.96). Capote uses personification to suggest that the fear experienced is out of hand, stating that 'imagination ... can open any door – turn the key and let terror walk right in' (p.96). The burial of the Clutters does not appear to ease the minds of the people either, and Capote's image of a thousand mourners reciting the Lord's Prayer 'together in a low whisper' (p.104) suggests an anxious huddle of people scared to raise their voices for fear that they, too, might incur the pain and suffering inflicted upon their friends. This notion is enhanced by the revelation that Dewey continuously receives calls from locals offering their theories on why the murders happened or 'nervous ladies alarmed by the gossip going around, rumours that knew neither ceiling nor cellar' (pp.108–9).

Alvin Dewey and 'three of the K.B.I.'s ablest investigators – Special Agents Harold Nye, Roy Church and Clarence Duntz' (p.88) are tasked with the responsibility of solving the case, and thus returning a sense of normality to the local community. With a confident and authoritative narrative voice, Capote deems Dewey's appointment to lead the investigation 'inevitable, and appropriate' (p.87) due to his extensive experience, and Dewey reveals a dogged determination to establish 'the why and the who' (p.88) of the Clutter murders. The question of 'why' proves difficult to answer because 'neither of the women had been "sexually molested"' and 'nothing had been stolen from the house' (p.89). Capote characterises Dewey in the manner of a hero in a Hollywood western, searching for patterns and connections in order to make sense of the crime which, due to the signs of 'twisted tenderness' (p.111) at the scene, suggests a 'psychopathic rage' (p.90). Dewey is also revealed to be cunning, withholding from the press the fact that the murderers left evidence in the form of footprints. This move proves to be significant. In seeking to solve the murder, Dewey is forced to rethink his ideas about the nature of evil and how a person comes to perpetrate apparently motiveless murders like those of the Clutters; as further 'meaningful developments' in the case occur, he realises that 'plain robbery' (p.110) might have been the sole motive.

Again using alternating yet contemporaneous narrative threads, Capote gives further insights into Dick and Perry and their relationship. Capote's masterful characterisation establishes Perry as a pathetic and pitiable character, thus inducing the reader to feel sympathy for him. For example, Capote suggests that Perry cannot put the crimes out of his mind and considers that 'there must be something wrong with us. To do what we did' (p.115). He also reveals that Perry had a difficult childhood, which led to a recurring dream of a big yellow parrot that 'had first flown into his dreams when he was seven years old, a hated, hating half-breed child living in a California orphanage run by nuns – shrouded disciplinarians who whipped him for wetting his bed' (p.100). The bird appears to be a 'warrior-angel' (p.101) that has, over the years, wrought vengeance in Perry's dreams on those who have caused him pain. This dream reveals Perry's deep emotional scars. There are hints to the reader that the damage might also be psychological, such as Dick's recognition that Perry's temper is such that 'he might be ready to kill you, but you'd never know it, not to look at or listen to'. Dick states that he 'felt he ought to be afraid of [Perry]', and Perry himself admits, 'I never thought I could do it. A thing like that' (p.116).

In contrast, Dick Hickock is characterised in a manner that arouses little, if any, sympathy. Capote encourages the reader to respond with fear to Dick's reaction when Perry raises the topic of Floyd Wells – the 'symptoms of fury' cause Dick's face to slacken and 'saliva bubbles' (p.99) appear at the corners of his mouth. Dick is also revealed to be 'smooth' and 'smart' (p.104), with 'perfect pitch' (p.105) when conning unsuspecting shopkeepers out of money by passing bad cheques, and he shows no remorse for his actions. Rather than responding sympathetically to Perry's concerns, he is instead 'annoyed as hell' and wonders 'why the hell couldn't Perry shut up ... Just forget it' (p.115). Dick is keen to assert that he is 'normal', yet he runs over a dog 'which was something he did whenever the opportunity arose'. The callousness of his exclamation, 'Boy! We sure splattered him!' inclines the reader to suspect that Dick is the one who carried out the violent murders (p.120).

The nature of the relationship between Dick and Perry is of interest here. As they engage in a honeymoon-like trip to Mexico City, Dick refers to Perry as 'baby' (p.98) and 'honey' (p.99), thus asserting his dominance over his feminised partner in crime. At the same time, Perry seems to be dependent on Dick, desperate for his friendship and his respect. Perry clings to his friendship with Dick so that he might live out his plans of 'a skin-diving, treasure-hunting life lived together among islands or along coasts south of the border' (p.99). Yet Perry's dreams of making his fortune are clearly going to be hampered by Dick's reluctance to go. Furthermore, Perry's dreams are unrealistic, though he seems incapable of recognising how ludicrous his idea of skippering a deep-sea-fishing boat is, given that he has never 'skippered a canoe or hooked a guppy' (p.107). Even in Mexico, when Perry comes near to achieving one of his most cherished fantasies, he is unable to take advantage of the moment because of humiliation about his body.

Key point

The comments (p.115) of Howard Fox, Bonnie Clutter's brother, regarding the death penalty suggest that salvation is a possibility for Perry and Dick. Consider the importance of Capote introducing this idea at this point in the narrative.

Key vocabulary

Bravura: a display of daring.

Prevarications: acting or speaking evasively.

Q Capote describes the photos of the slain family from Dewey's perspective in detail. What narrative purpose do these graphic descriptions serve?

Q In what ways is Holcomb changed by the murder of the Clutter family?

Part 2: Persons Unknown (pp.130–61)

Summary: *Dick and Perry run out of money and decide to return to the United States. Perry sorts through his belongings. Dewey works himself to exhaustion trying to solve the case.*

After a short period in Acapulco and Mexico City, the decision to return to the United States is made by Dick, whose callous nature is evident when he tells Perry to 'wake up' because 'there ain't no caskets of gold' (p.131). Perry continues to demonstrate a pathological dependence on Dick, unwilling to part from him even though he had always been 'a loner' (p.131). As he packs his possessions, Perry displays a distorted sense of right and wrong in his bitterness about the theft of his guitar, despite his lack of qualms about stealing from the Clutters and the shops in Kansas City. The mementos Perry selects from his 'old letters, photographs, clippings' (p.132) are important as they enhance the reader's understanding of him.

The first memento Perry selects is the 'badly typed composition' (p.132) written by his father, Tex John Smith, which prompts him to feel 'a stable of emotions' including 'self-pity ..., love and hate' (p.137). The letter is followed by an extended biography of Perry written from the viewpoint of the omniscient narrator and littered with quotes from the subject himself. Both Perry's father's written account and the subsequent biography make it clear that Perry had a horrific childhood. Rejected by his alcoholic mother, Perry was deprived of access to an education, and it appears he never experienced the emotional intimacy and security with another human that is crucial to a person's development, for when he sought help from his father, he simply 'told [Perry] to be good and hugged [him] and went away' (p.139). Perry's subsequent placement in a Catholic orphanage saw him being hit by the 'Black Widows' (p.139) for wetting the bed; he was then placed in a children's shelter run by the Salvation Army where he was exposed to even worse abuses, which taught him the 'evil' (p.139) of which people are capable. The life of abuse continued for Perry in the Merchant Marines, where 'the queens on ship wouldn't leave me alone' (p.140); 'the same problem came up' (p.141) years later when he was in the army. The family member who might have helped Perry recover from this abuse, his sister Barbara, also rejects him, telling Perry he cannot blame others for his childhood and must take responsibility. Through the inclusion of Willie-Jay's analysis of Barbara's letter, Capote provides a subtle clue as to the motive behind Perry's killing of the Clutters, as his analysis that 'letters like this ... *can only serve to increase your already dangerous anti-social instincts*' (p.151) suggests that family is a catalyst for Perry's easily triggered temper. Capote thus portrays a damaged person who never had a chance in life.

The narrative returns to Alvin Dewey, revealing the toll that the case is taking on him and his team. He has 'lost twenty pounds' and yet is in 'better shape' than other members of his team (p.155) due to their tireless efforts to solve the case. The community's demands for a resolution are such that Dewey has become a target of 'abuse' from locals who demand that he 'arrest somebody' because 'that's what you're paid for' (p.156). Such abuse reveals the continued fear and uncertainty that plague Holcomb and Garden City. The difficulty of the case is highlighted by the simile describing earlier murder cases that Dewey has worked on as 'squalls preceding a hurricane' (p.158). But Capote also reveals that Dewey has excellent instincts, as his suspicions are closer to the truth than he realises.

Part 2 closes with Dick and Perry hitchhiking on Route 66, Dick full of joy at being back in America, but also with a clear intention to kill again.

Key point

Capote's characterisation of Perry humanises a man viewed by society as an animal. By evoking sympathy for Perry because of his difficult childhood, Capote prepares the reader to be willing to consider that the justice system must recognise the impact of the past on Perry's actions as an adult.

Q Why might Capote have chosen to include the letters from Perry's father and sister, and from Willie-Jay? Why didn't Capote edit the documents before putting them in the book?

Q In view of the revelation that there have been murders in Holcomb before, are the fears of the locals reasonable? Consider the psychological needs behind the community's desire for answers.

Part 3: Answer (pp.162–214)

Summary: *Floyd Wells informs authorities of Dick and Perry's identities. Dewey is hopeful of catching the murderers. Harold Nye speaks with Dick's parents, Perry's former landlady, and Perry's sister. Dick and Perry pass through Kansas to write more bad cheques then go to Miami for Christmas, before heading to Las Vegas.*

As indicated by the title, the search for an answer underlies this section. Part 3 begins with Floyd Wells, the 'single connexion' (p.98) that Perry spoke of in Part 2. The negativity with which Capote characterises Wells positions the reader to view him as untrustworthy, thus bringing into question the reliability of his subsequent testimony. Wells is 'nearly chinless' and 'had attempted several careers' including that of 'thief' (p.162). His claim to have liked Herb Clutter 'much as any man I ever met' (p.163) seems at odds with the fact that he 'can't honestly say I tried to persuade [Dick]' (pp.164–5) out of robbing and killing the family. Furthermore, Capote questions Wells' decision to delay informing authorities of Dick's identity, labelling his situation 'curious, his excuses questionable' (p.165), thus suggesting that Wells is speaking out only in the hope of a reduced sentence and a cash reward. Regardless of the validity of Well's information, it directs the attention of the authorities to Dick and Perry, and the manhunt for the killers begins. As the KBI team comes closer to locating them, Capote's language creates a heightened sense of anticipation that an arrest might occur, as a 'quivering stillness now permeated the premises' and members of the KBI team are 'like huntsmen hiding in a forest … afraid that any abrupt sound or movement would warn away approaching beasts' (p.193).

Key point

The reader gazes upon the police photographs of the killers through the viewpoint of Dewey's wife Marie. She considers Smith to be 'tough, yet not entirely' and 'sensitive' but also 'mean'. She judges Hickock the more 'forbiddingly criminal', his eyes filling her 'with terror' (p.167).

The 'beasts', of course, are Dick and Perry, and further information on their backgrounds is provided from various viewpoints in order to shape the reader's feelings towards the two characters. The majority of the information in this section is garnered by Harold Nye, one of the KBI detectives working on the investigation. The impression given of Dick is of a selfish, ruthless man filled with envy and greed. Nye's meeting with Dick's parents reveals that, though they 'never have had any money', they both 'love him' (p.168) and have provided him with a stable, supportive home environment, a fact to which locals attest. Mr Hickock suggests that it was Dick's car accident that set him on a criminal path, that after the accident 'he wasn't the same boy', and that time in Lansing further changed his son to the point that when he came out, 'he was a plain stranger to me' (p.169). The most condemnatory revelations about Dick occur while he and Perry are in Miami at Christmastime. The depth of Dick's sociopathy is revealed through the personification of 'Envy', which has been 'constantly with him' (p.203) since childhood, and his capacity for violence is revealed through the authoritative statement from the narrator, framed so that it sounds like Dick's thoughts, that 'with a knife in his hand, he ... had power' (p.204). Dick's claim to be 'normal' is also undermined, as he rationalises his desire for under-age girls by arguing that 'most real men had the same desires' (p.204).

While Capote's depiction of Perry continues to be more forgiving that that of Dick, insights into Perry's darker side are introduced. When the two men plan to murder Mr Bell, a travelling salesman who unsuspectingly picks them up when they are hitchhiking, Perry's response to the fact that Bell has five children is simply, 'well, too bad' (p.175), hinting at a callous disdain for human life. Furthermore, Perry's irritation at Bell's 'hearty barks that sounded very much like the laughter of Tex John Smith' (p.176) again suggests that Perry's past may be at the root of his damaged psyche, a fact reinforced by the revelation by Perry's sister, Barbara Johnson, that Perry believed he was simply his father's 'nigger ... Somebody he could work their guts out and never have to pay them' (p.188). Barbara reveals she is 'afraid of [Perry]', because 'he has no respect for anyone' (p.184) and her statement that 'he can fool you. He can make you feel so sorry for him' (p.185) serves as a warning to the reader of Perry's complex and pathological nature. Yet the contradictory elements of Perry's character are clear. It is revealed that he has 'no respect for people who can't control themselves sexually' (p.204) and, in the episode in which Dick and Perry pick up the young boy and his dying grandfather, Perry demonstrates a significant degree of empathy towards the pair.

Key vocabulary

Ambivalent: having mixed feelings or contradictory ideas about something or someone.

Ominous: signalling evil; threatening.

Querulous: prone to complaining.

Somnolent: sleepy or drowsy.

Q Why is Perry's violence directed at 'respectable' people?

Part 3: Answer (pp.214–51)

Summary: *On 30 December 1959, Dick and Perry are apprehended in Las Vegas. The KBI team goes to Las Vegas to interrogate the suspects. Dick makes a full confession, blaming the murders on Perry; Perry makes a full confession, blaming the murder of the women on Dick. Holcomb responds to the arrests and a crowd gathers in Garden City as the suspects are brought in.*

Luck is revealed to be on the side of the KBI when Dick and Perry are arrested in Las Vegas – the package Perry collects from the Las Vegas post office contains the boots that will become key evidence in the case against the two. When being interrogated, Dick initially exudes confidence because of his carefully crafted alibi and his belief that he has only been picked up for a parole violation. But when the Clutter murder is raised, he is quick to proclaim, 'I'm no goddam killer' (p.225). In this scene, Capote examines the methods used by the investigators to trap the suspects and force a confession, skilfully dramatising the pressure they apply and Dick's wavering between confessing and withholding information. His decision to confess is ultimately made because of Nye and Church's revelation that there is 'a living witness' (p.225).

The most significant moment in this section is Perry Smith's confession, and Capote highlights this with a shift from past tense to the present continuous tense, signifying that the dual narrative threads have come together. While the narrative to this point has done much to elicit sympathy for Perry because of his traumatic past, the depiction of the killings is horrific and confronting. Capote uses a technique considered controversial in terms of the nonfiction novel form: instead of quoting directly or using typical journalistic attribution, his use of omniscient point of view suggests access to Perry's private thoughts. There appears to be a dissociation between Perry's thoughts and emotions and his actions throughout his account of the night of 14 November. He suggests that, rather than going to the Clutters' house with malicious intention, he merely 'let [him]self be carried along', though he also admits that he 'wanted the money as much as [Dick] did' (p.236). There are moments of hesitation that suggest that the tide of events that night might have gone differently, and it is apparent that the Clutters, Herb in particular, were compliant because they could not conceive of the evil Dick and Perry were ultimately proved capable of. From Perry's account, it appears that Dick drives the events, even when it is clear there is no money, because of his desire to rape Nancy and his excitement at the 'glory of having everybody at his mercy' (p.241). Perry's 'ironic, erratic compassion' (p.243), which continues right up until the moment he begins murdering the family, is difficult to reconcile with his actions. During the act of murder he appears to be completely disconnected from the moment, claiming, 'I didn't realize what I'd done' (p.247).

Dewey's response to Perry's confession is important. Society's inability to understand the behaviour of the criminally insane is evident in Dewey's dissatisfaction and disappointment with the confessions because, 'though they answered questions of how and why, [they] failed to satisfy his sense of meaningful design' (p.248). The answers do not provide Dewey with a satisfactory motive, nor does he believe the deaths have affected the consciences of the criminals, and for this reason he desires retribution, to see 'Perry and his partner hanged – hanged back to back' (p.248). Thus, with the close of this section, the reader's anticipation shifts now to the execution of the killers, whom the people of Holcomb are stunned to discover are 'humanly shaped' (p.251).

Key point

It is sheer luck that leads to Perry's confession; he remains silent until Dewey reveals that Dick told the detectives Perry's story about murdering King with a bicycle chain, a story that Dick does not realise is a fabrication. This revelation signifies to Perry that the detectives are telling the truth – that Dick has made a confession.

Key vocabulary

Expurgated: having offensive material removed.

Fusillade: a general discharge or outpouring.

Q How do Dewey's reactions to Perry's confession affect the reader?

Q Members of the local community 'feel disappointed at being told that the murderer was not someone among themselves' (p.233). Why do you think they are 'disappointed'?

Part 4: The Corner (pp.252–308)

Summary: *Dick and Perry are kept in separate jail cells in Garden City awaiting trial. Perry wishes to alter his confession. The Clutter estate is auctioned off. Dick and Perry are tried and convicted of murder, and sentenced to the death penalty.*

The housing of Perry in the 'ladies' cell' (p.252) builds upon a thread developed by Capote throughout the narrative in which Perry is feminised, thus softening the reader's perception of him and making him less threatening. The observations of Mrs Josie Meier continue to give Perry a distinctly human face as he tends to his appearance and 'sketched portraits' and 'drew flowers' (p.255), yet his capacity for evil is equally evident when he malevolently says of his sister, 'I wish she'd been in that house that night. What a sweet scene!' (p.260). A poignant moment occurs when Perry observes 'two thin grey toms' (p.264) in the square below his cell who are 'hunting for dead birds caught in the vehicles' engine grilles'. Perry's inability to look at them because 'most of my life I've done what they're doing' (p.265) reminds the reader that Perry's life has been hard, and thus continues to emphasise that he is both pitiable and pathetic. This moment is the clearest of several in the text in which Capote draws an explicit connection between Perry and various animals in exile, animals that are products of their environment. Interestingly, Capote's characterisation of Dick becomes more nuanced in this section, as Dick is observed not to be the 'unusually untroubled young man' (p.263) that others perceive him to be, though he continues to show little regard for the lives of others. Additionally, the inclusion of Dick and Perry's autographical accounts allows the reader to view their lives and circumstances from their perspectives and provides significant material for a consideration of the theme of nature versus nurture.

Key point

The simile describing Perry entering the court looking 'as lonely and inappropriate as a seagull in a wheat field' (p.273) accentuates his alienation and isolation.

Given the confessions made by both Dick and Perry and the evidence collected by the KBI team, the state has an 'unshakeable case' (p.257) as the matter goes to trial. Although there is no doubt of Dick and Perry's guilt, Capote now turns a critical eye on the fairness of the justice system. At each stage it is clear that Capote believes the county is ensuring that the death penalty will be given. Dick's father observes that, 'the way folks feel, [Dick] don't stand no chance' (p.260). Capote pointedly brings into question the impartiality of the witnesses, which is further compromised by Judge Tate's decision to allow them to view the 'death-scene images' (p.280). These make the jurors 'angry' to the point that 'several of them ... stared at the defendants with total contempt' (p.281). The validity of Wells' testimony, 'perfected by pre-trial rehearsal', is also scrutinised, Capote making it clear that Wells is far from 'trustworthy' (p.282) in terms of establishing premeditation.

The decision by Judge Tate to deny the defence request for 'comprehensive psychiatric examinations for the accused' (p.267) means that the determination as to whether the two men can be held legally responsible for their crime is left in the hands of 'local physicians' (p.268) rather than experts in criminal psychiatry. Furthermore, when Dr Jones, a 'sophisticated specialist in criminal psychology and the criminally insane' (p.269) takes the stand to discuss Dick and Perry's culpability, he is prevented from presenting his opinion due to the restrictions of the M'Naughten Rule. The unfairness of this is pointed out through the intrusion of Capote's authorial voice advising that the M'Naughten formula is 'quite colour-blind to any permutations between black and white' and renders Dr Jones 'impotent' (p.293). In the guise of impartiality and neutrality, Capote expresses his belief that the justice system's use of the M'Naughten Rule is inappropriate. By then including Dr Jones' findings regarding both Dick and Perry, and reinforcing the validity of these findings with the inclusion of Dr Satten's article on criminal psychology, Capote provides the men with the trial he believes they should have had.

Key point

The diagnoses of Dick as suffering from 'a severe character disorder' (p.295) and Perry as possibly being 'paranoid schizophrenic' (p.298) directly challenge the validity of the M'Naughten Rule, which reduces the determination of whether a person 'knew right from wrong at the time of the commission of the crime' (p.293) to a simple 'yes' or 'no' answer.

A significant event in this section is the auction of the Clutter estate on 21 March 1960. Capote's purpose in including this event is twofold. The first and most obvious reason is that, as Defence Attorney Harrison Smith argues, the 'auction of the victim's estate' a week before the trial's commencement is 'prejudicial' (p.269) and will impact on the impartiality of prospective jurors. The second purpose is a veiled condemnation of the avaricious nature of society. The auction draws 'more than five thousand people' and, while some of them come 'out of curiosity' (p.270), most are there for the opportunity to buy 'merchandise at bargain prices'. This sad moment, which is like a 'second funeral' (p.271) for those close to the Clutters, simultaneously highlights the ephemeral nature of life and the materialistic greed of middle America, as members of this demographic profit from the murders just as Dick and Perry sought to.

Key point

The masterful and highly manipulative closing arguments of prosecuting attorney Logan Green are the culminating point of the unfair trial, and Green's appeal to the jurors' fear when he states that 'the next time they go slaughtering it may be *your* family' (p.305) means that Dick and Perry 'don't stand a chance' (p.306).

Key vocabulary

Dissociative: relating to dissociation (the splitting off of certain mental processes from the conscious mind).

Habitués: regular frequenters of a place.

Melange: a mixture or medley.

Pugnacious: prone to fighting; aggressive.

Sartorially: relating to clothes or dress.

Unctuous: excessively smooth or suave.

Venire: a panel from which a jury is drawn.

Vicissitudes: variations; alternating phases or conditions in the course of something.

Voir dire: the preliminary examination of a prospective witness or juror to establish their competence.

Q The opening words of Part 4 are 'institutional dourness' (p.252). How does this set the tone for this final section?

Q Perry indicates that he wishes to change his statement to claim responsibility for killing all four members of the Clutter family. Do you believe that Perry killed the whole family, or do you think he takes responsibility 'out of consideration for Hickock's parents' (p.256), as Dewey suggests?

Part 4: The Corner (pp.308–43)

Summary: *Dick and Perry are sent to Death Row ('the Corner'). Dick lodges multiple appeals but after five years he and Perry are hanged on 15 April 1965. Dewey attends the hanging and recalls a (fictional) encounter with Susan Kidwell a year earlier.*

The closing section of the book is notable for its morbid tone and images of institutionalisation. As the prisoners enter 'Death Row', which is housed at Lansing Prison in a building 'shaped like a coffin', they are 'stripped, showered, given close haircuts, and supplied with coarse denim uniforms and soft slippers' (p.309) then housed in cells with windows 'covered with a wire mesh black as a widow's veil' (p.310). Here, Dick and Perry join a small group of criminals also condemned to death. The stories of these inmates, particularly that of Lowell Lee Andrews, provide further insight into questions regarding justice, morality, mental health and the nature of evil.

Key point

The footwear given to the prisoners on Death Row – slippers – is intended to prevent inmates taking their own lives. The state ensures that only it can take the lives of those on Death Row so that the opportunity for retribution is not lost.

Dick and Perry remain on Death Row for approximately five years, their lives extended by numerous stays of execution while appeals are heard. During this time, Perry goes on a hunger strike and his mental health deteriorates substantially as he hears voices. Significantly, one of Perry's hallucinations takes on a religious tone and he wakes up shouting, 'The bird is Jesus! The bird is Jesus!' (p.319). This revelation reinforces Capote's contention that Perry suffered from significant mental trauma, and therefore supports the idea that his sanity at the time of the murders is in doubt. This calls into question the appropriateness of the death penalty. Ironically, Perry's anger at his father, which seems to have spurred him to kill Herb Clutter, gives him the will to end his hunger strike and live. Dick's suffering differs from Perry's at this time – his dreams shift from fantasies of wealth and women to a fantasy that he might escape the hangman's noose, and he remains adamant that he is 'no goddam killer' (p.326).

Ultimately, the appeals fail, and Dick and Perry are executed. Capote's descriptions of the executions support arguments against the death penalty. The reader, through Dewey's viewpoint, is placed in the room with the noose and the hangman, and must observe the brutality of the deaths. Dewey notes that the execution chamber lacks the 'suitable dignity' (p.337) he expected, and finds the 'casual conversations of his fellow witnesses ... disconcerting' (p.338). This scene seems to reinforce Perry's suggestion to Don Cullivan that it is 'possible for any man' to kill without 'conscience or compassion' (p.290) and thus suggests that the death penalty is simply a state-sanctioned 'ritual of vengeance' (p.339) performed in the same 'cold blood' with which Dick and Perry murdered the Clutters. Capote strips away the notion that being hanged is free from cruelty: Dick is not pronounced dead for 'a full twenty minutes' (p.339) and one of the onlookers believes he 'could hear him gasping for breath' (p.340). Capote uses the scene of Perry's execution to make a final statement against the death penalty by having Perry condemn capital punishment. The descriptions of Perry here harken back to earlier in the text, with references to his 'sensitive eyes' (p.340) and 'childish feet'. Thus the final image of Perry is one of lost potential and suffering, while Dewey finds that he does not have the 'sense of climax, release' (p.341) that he thought the deaths would bring.

Key point

Capote's own weariness with the case is evident at this point, and the narrative viewpoint suggests an emotional distance from the killers that was not previously evident. It should be noted that Capote had essentially finished the book long before the murderers were hanged – all his book lacked was an ending. He was therefore in a morally fraught position, waiting for the men he had befriended to die so that he could finish, and publish, his book.

Key point

The authenticity of Capote's account of Perry's last words was disputed by numerous witnesses at the hanging. It has been argued that Capote scripted these words to make Perry a redeemable and sympathetic character.

Capote wanted to end with something happier than the execution of the killers, and therefore made the oft-criticised decision to conclude with an invented meeting between Alvin Dewey and Susan Kidwell in a cemetery. Told through Dewey's perspective, the point of this scene is that even after a terrible murder, life goes on: people continue to be absorbed by their own preoccupations. The wind provides a poetic ending to the grim tale of crime and punishment on the plains of Kansas, and ends the story with a sense of peace.

Key vocabulary

Jaunty: easy and sprightly in manner.

Malodorous: having a bad smell.

Phlegmatic: cool or self-possessed.

Q What parallels can you identify between Dick and Perry and the other inmates on Death Row?

CHARACTERS & RELATIONSHIPS

Perry Edward Smith

Key quotes

'You are a man of extreme passion ... a deeply frustrated man striving to project his individuality against a backdrop of rigid conformity.' (Willie-Jay, p.54)

'Oh, he can fool you. He can make you feel so sorry for him.' (Barbara Johnson, p.185)

'I'm embraced by shame.' (p.308)

Perry Edward Smith was born on 27 October 1928 in Huntington, Nevada. Physically, Perry seems to be composed of mismatched parts, with the 'torso of a weight-lifter' yet 'stunted legs' and 'tiny feet' that seem 'grotesquely inadequate' (p.27) to the task of supporting his muscular frame. This representation of Perry's physical form presages the revelation of his dual nature, a nature that seems to be a consequence of his traumatic past.

Perry is the fourth child of an Irish father, 'Tex' John Smith, and a Cherokee mother, Julie 'Flo' Buckskin. Prior to revealing the chilling details of the murder of the Clutters, Capote gradually reveals Perry's childhood to have been traumatic, thus positioning the reader to feel sympathy for the killer. Much like Capote himself, Perry was scarred by his parents' neglect. His father was capable of violent outbursts and, as a boy, Perry witnessed Tex 'beating [his] mother' (p.274) until she left him. Perry's mother was a drunk and 'never in a fit condition to properly provide and care for' her children. Perry became a juvenile delinquent and ended up in 'Detention Homes' (p.275) where he was assaulted by those responsible for his care. Both in the marines and in the army he appears to have been subjected to sexual abuse. Perry's desire for escape from his traumatic past is revealed by his recurring dream of a big yellow bird that, over the years, delivers him from a series of torments.

Rather than being a one-dimensional maniacal killer, Perry is depicted as an artistic man filled with dreams of wealth and fame. His ability to 'sympathize' (p.35) with Dick's parents for hating him reveals a capacity for emotional sensitivity. He dreams of 'singing ... in front of an audience' (p.28) and is 'an incessant conceiver of voyages' (p.26), but Perry's past seems to have put a series of insurmountable barriers in front of him, leaving him no legitimate means for actualising his desires. His life is 'an ugly and lonely progress towards one mirage and then another' (p.248) and his pursuit of these mirages ultimately brings him to the Clutter household on 14 November.

Key point

Capote's complex depiction of Perry suggests the author's belief that, rather than seeking to categorise people as good or bad, sane or insane, society – and the legal system in particular – should treat people with compassion and understanding, recognising that their formative experiences can have a tragic impact upon the course of their lives.

Perry and Willie-Jay

Willie-Jay is considered by Perry to be his 'real and only friend' and it is a reunion with him that Perry wants 'more than anything in the world'. Having been so often rejected throughout his life, Perry's friendship with Willie-Jay appears to have the potential to be a salve for Perry's wounded psyche, for Willie-Jay views Perry as a 'poet, something rare and savable' (p.53), a view that aligns with how Perry sees himself.

Perry and authority figures

Key quotes

'You think I *like* myself? Oh, the man I could have been! But that bastard never gave me a chance.' (p.188)

'I wonder why I did it ... it wasn't because of anything the Clutters did. They never hurt me. Like other people. Like people have all my life. Maybe it's just that the Clutters were the ones who had to pay for it.' (p.290)

According to both Dr Jones and Dr Satten, the cycle of violence and rejection that marked Perry's relationship with his father and his subsequent abuse at the hands of those with authority over him were central to Perry's trauma. Authority figures tend to bring out 'violent assaultive behaviour' (p.297) in Perry, but that behaviour seems to occur within 'a schizophrenic darkness' (p.302) in which Perry has no control over his actions. Capote contends that the Clutters did not die because of anything they did, but because of the things that had been done by others in the past.

Richard Eugene Hickock

Key quotes

'Deal me out, baby. I'm a normal.' (p.118)

'A cinch ... I promise you, honey, we'll blast hair all over them walls.' (p.34)

'Envy was constantly with him; the Enemy was anyone who was someone he wanted to be or who had anything he wanted to have.' (p.203)

Richard 'Dick' Hickock was born on 6 June 1931 in Kansas City, Kansas. His parents, though poor, are 'plain, honest people' (p.171) who provided Dick with a happy childhood. Their only fault, it seems, is poverty, which prevented them from sending Dick to college because they 'plain didn't have the money' (p.168). Perhaps because he viewed Dick as the less interesting subject of the killer duo, Capote gives few further details about Dick's past. He does note that Dick has been 'twice married, twice divorced', is 'the father of three boys' (p.35) and has 'imperfectly aligned features' (p.42) as a consequence of a 1950 car accident.

Dick is portrayed in a predominantly negative manner, ostensibly through the eyes of Perry. He is presented as both ruthless and remorseless, characteristics that set him in sharp contrast to the sensitive Perry. In the six weeks that he and Perry are on the run, Dick gives little indication that he is upset by the murders, expressing frustration that Perry will not 'just forget it' (p.115). Capote takes great pains to regularly reveal Dick's sociopathic tendencies, depicting such behaviours as his running over a dog, passing bad cheques, and planning the Clutter murders 'from first footfall to final silence' (p.48). He is also revealed to have paedophilic tendencies. Dr Jones suggests that underlying Dick's hatred and aggression are deep-seated feelings of being 'inferior to others and sexually inadequate' (p.294). This suggestion is reinforced by Perry's revelation that when Dick is having sex he can be heard incessantly whispering 'as though reciting a rosary', 'Is it good, baby? Is it good?' (p.153), as well as by the narrator's claim that 'with a knife in his hand, he, Dick, had power' (p.204). Dick likes to repeatedly declare that he is 'normal'. But Capote characterises him as a manipulative man whose 'truly serpentine' (p.42) eye reveals more about his true nature than he is willing to acknowledge.

Key point

Though there is doubt as to whether Dick actually killed any of the Clutters, neither Dewey nor Capote exhibit any qualms that he is sent to the gallows for the crime.

Dick and Perry

Though Dick and Perry each express a dislike of the other at various stages in the narrative, the two seem to be drawn to each other. They are, as Perry says, 'of the same species, brothers in the breed of Cain' (p.261). For Dick, Perry is someone who can be 'profitably exploited' (p.66) in order to deliver him his dreams and desires, while Perry is 'attracted' to Dick because he is 'totally masculine' (p.28), though this attraction wanes as he realises that Dick is 'a blowhard' (p.196).

Alvin Dewey

Key quotes

'For Dewey, himself a former sheriff of Finney county (from 1947 to 1955) and, prior to that, a Special Agent of the F.B.I. ... was professionally qualified to cope with even as intricate an affair as the apparently motiveless, all but clueless Clutter murders.' (pp.87–8)

'I'm haunted by them. I guess I always will be. Until I know what happened.' (p.154)

A 'lean and handsome fourth-generation Kansan of forty-seven' (p.87), Alvin Dewey quickly emerges as the hero of Capote's story. Dewey appears to have a loving bond with his wife Marie and two sons, and this, combined with his professional qualifications, not only makes his appointment 'appropriate' (p.87) but also establishes him as a man of principles whom the reader can trust. The fact that Dewey was 'real fond of Herb and Bonnie' makes the case personal for him, but it is the violence of the murders that drives him to find out 'the why and the who' (p.88).

Dewey pursues the case to the detriment of his own health and wellbeing, becoming uncharacteristically absent-minded as his mind 'rejected problems not concerned with the Clutter case' (p.154). He becomes 'emaciated' and is 'smoking sixty cigarettes a day' (p.167) as he chases down every possible lead, because he fears the case will remain 'in the Open File' (p.154) and prevent him from ever being able to move beyond the murders of his friends. Furthermore, Dewey must contend with townspeople haranguing him about the case, as they, too, seem unable to move forward in their lives until it is solved.

Ultimately, Dewey's patience and thoroughness, combined with some exceptional moments of good luck, allow him to catch the killers, and his testimony at the trial makes him 'the prosecution's most damaging witness' (p.285). His reflections at the hangings of Dick and Perry are therefore all the more important as, while the reader might anticipate that Dewey, as an advocate of the death penalty, will feel 'a sense of climax, release, of a design justly completed', he instead closes his eyes and appears unsettled by the sight of Perry's 'childish feet, tilted, dangling' (p.341).

Key point

Dewey's character is an essential vehicle for Capote to convey his own views and values. Dewey's ability to carefully consider every facet of a situation establishes him as reliable and trustworthy, and thus inclines the reader to agree with his observations.

Herbert William Clutter

Key quote

'Always certain of what he wanted from the world, Mr. Clutter had in large measure obtained it.' (p.18)

Perhaps because he never met the man, Capote's characterisation of Herb Clutter is markedly static in *In Cold Blood*. Forty-eight-year-old Herb is the epitome of success, a 'man's man' (p.17) who, through hard work and dedication, has realised the American dream. Everything about Herb exudes strength and confidence, from his 'broad' shoulders and 'square-jawed, confident face' (p.17) to his 'fearless self-assurance' (p.47).

Capote characterises Herb as a 'captain' of industry who navigates 'River Valley's sometimes risky passage through the seasons' (p.30). Herb is a strict yet loving father and a devoted husband to his troubled wife. Even in his final moments, when threatened at gunpoint by Dick, Herb exhibits love and tenderness towards his wife, telling her, 'It's all right, sweetheart. Don't be afraid' (p.240).

Herb's name is 'everywhere respectfully recognized' (p.18) due to the many groups he is involved in, which include the Methodist Church, the Finney County 4-H Club and a role as 'chairman of the Kansas Conference of Farm Organizations' (pp.17–18). Locals struggle to understand why someone might have killed Herb, for he was known for 'his equanimity, his charitableness, and the fact that he paid good wages and distributed frequent bonuses' (p.22). From Perry's confession and the opinions of Dr Satten and Dr Jones, it appears that Herb's death is ultimately not a result of anything he has done as an individual, but because of what he represents: authority.

Key point

Herb's death signifies the tenuous nature of success, and is unsettling to locals, who feel that his many acts of kindness and generosity ought to have been defence enough against the horrors wrought upon him and his family by the killers.

Bonnie Clutter

Key quotes

'She was "nervous", she suffered "little spells" ... everyone knew she had been an on-and-off psychiatric patient the last half-dozen years.' (p.18)

'But she was not without hope. Trust in God sustained her, and from time to time secular sources supplemented her faith in His forthcoming mercy.' (p.39)

Married to Herb Clutter for twenty-five years, Bonnie Clutter is a reclusive woman who in many ways seems the antithesis of her husband. Bonnie's childhood is said to have been a 'lovely' one, in which she was not 'spoiled' but 'spared, led to suppose that life was a sequence of agreeable events' (p.37). But 'maturity ... ha[s] reduced her voice to a single tone, that of apology' and Bonnie is viewed as 'slightly odd, but *nice*' (p.36). Capote seems to imply that marriage and motherhood are largely responsible for Bonnie's mental health issues, which began with 'an inexplicable despondency' following the birth of her first child and manifested as a 'mood of misery' that 'never altogether lifted' after Kenyon was born. The simile used to describe Bonnie's depressions – 'like a cloud that might rain or might not' (p.38) – suggests her moods are unpredictable and uncontrollable.

Key point

Society's treatment of Bonnie's mental health issues should be contrasted with the treatment of Perry's. Before the details of the murders are known, Nancy Kidwell's mother exclaims, 'Oh Bonnie, Bonnie, what happened? ... you said you'd never be sick again' (p.72), implying that Bonnie's depression was such that others considered her capable of committing a murder-suicide.

Herb and Bonnie's marriage

Key quote

> 'On his left hand, on what remained of a finger once mangled by a piece of farm machinery, he wore a plain gold band, which was the symbol ... of his marriage to the person he had wished to marry.' (p.18)

On the surface, the Clutters appear to have a secure marriage, but Capote implies that the couple maintain an appearance of togetherness in public in order to conform to societal expectations. That Herb's ring finger is 'mangled' can be read as symbolic of the damage his determination to succeed in life has done to his marriage. This notion is reinforced by the revelation that Bonnie sleeps in a separate room from Herb, as well as the authorial comment that the couple had gone 'their semi-separate ways' (p.38). Capote is perhaps suggesting society deceives itself, imagining a perfection that never truly exists.

Nancy Clutter

Key quotes

> 'She's got *character*. Gets it from her old man.' (p.29)
>
> 'She was really nice. A very pretty girl, and not spoiled or anything.' (Perry, p.245)

When first introduced to the reader, sixteen-year-old Nancy, 'Barefoot' and 'pyjama-clad' (p.29), is the picture of adolescent innocence as she runs down the stairs to speak on the telephone. Like her father, Nancy seems to be a confident and kind person who contributed to the functioning of the Clutter household while also managing to be 'a straight-A student, the president of her class, a leader in the 4-H programme and the Young Methodists League, a skilled rider, an excellent musician ..., an annual winner at the county fair' (p.29). The only point of contention between Nancy and her father is the fact that her boyfriend, Bobby Rupp, is a Catholic and she is a Methodist (an insurmountable difference for a traditionalist like Herb), but it is likely that, even in that matter, she would eventually have acquiesced and split up with Bobby; as a dutiful daughter, she states, 'I just want to ... do as he wishes' (p.32).

Nancy is a young woman with much to give, though her adult identity is not yet fully formed, as symbolised by her experiments with handwriting in her diary, 'slanting it to the right or to the left, shaping it roundly or steeply, loosely or stingily – as though she were asking, "Is this Nancy? Or that? Or that? Which is me?"' (p.67).

Key point

While the reader is filled with sorrow at the lost potential of Nancy's young life, Capote takes great pains throughout the rest of the narrative to reveal how much of Perry's potential was also lost.

Kenyon Clutter

Key quote

'[I]n temperament he was not in the least Mr Clutter's son but rather Bonnie's child, a sensitive and reticent boy.' (p.51)

Fifteen-year-old Kenyon receives the least character development of all the members of the Clutter family. He is revealed to be a markedly different child to Nancy, preferring to be 'alone' (p.49), completing woodworking projects such as the 'cedar chest' (p.244) he made as a wedding present for his sister and spending time with 'guns, horses, tools, machinery, even a book' (p.51).

THEMES, IDEAS & VALUES

The American dream: fact or fantasy?

Key quotes

'Since childhood, for more than half his thirty-one years, he had been sending off for literature ... that stoked a longing to realize an adventure his imagination swiftly and over and over enabled him to experience.' (p.28)

'How was it possible that such effort, such plain virtue, could overnight be reduced to this – smoke, thinning as it rose and was received by the big, annihilating sky?' (p.87)

'All they want is some money.' (Herb, p.242)

In the 1950s, many Americans believed that their country was an exceptional place, a 'land of opportunity' that allowed individuals the chance to escape their environments if they wished, and that the determiner of any American's success was the content of their character. This belief in social mobility is an integral aspect of the American dream. Capote's portrayal of both the Clutter family and the Clutter killers suggests that the American dream is just that: merely a dream.

To all outside appearances, the Clutter family represent the achievement of the American dream. The family's successes arise from a commitment to their community and a willingness to work hard. As morally upright and deeply religious people, they are viewed by their community as deserving of their success. However, Capote insinuates that the perfection of this family is a myth: Herb and Bonnie have separate bedrooms, Bonnie struggles with depression, Nancy's relationship with Bobby is met with disapproval from her father, and Kenyon seems to prefer the isolation of the basement to interacting with his peers. If happiness and fulfilment evade even a family like the Clutters, then perhaps the American dream is simply an illusion.

While the portrayal of the Clutter family casts doubt over the validity of the American dream, the lives of Dick and Perry shatter it. Both Dick and Perry have lived in poverty, with little opportunity for social mobility. Even though Dick was an 'outstanding athlete' and a 'pretty good student', he was unable to attend college because his parents 'plain didn't have the money' (p.168). Perry's opportunities were even more limited, for he was denied the opportunity to attend school by his father, who 'didn't want [him] to learn anything' (p.188). Capote contends that 'class distinctions are as clearly observed, and as clearly observable' in Kansas as they are 'in any other human hive' (p.45). The barriers to entry into the middle class prove too high to scale for men like Dick and Perry. As a consequence, they see a life of criminality as the only way to achieve their dreams of wealth and glory, even if it means, as Perry says, 'crawling on my belly to steal a child's silver dollar' (p.242).

The lost innocence of a sheltered community

Key quotes

'[D]rama, in the shape of exceptional happenings, had never stopped there.' (p.17)

'I'll bet he *wasn't* afraid. I mean, however it happened, I'll bet right up to the last minute he didn't believe it would. Because it couldn't. Not to him.' (Mrs Ashida, p.124)

By writing his story from within the community of Garden City and its 'suburb', Holcomb, Capote is able to reveal the significant impact the crime had on middle America. The people of this area are 'prosperous' (p.16), and the sense of community and 'contentment' they feel means that 'animals and children are safe to run free' (p.45); in something of a cliché, the people are 'sufficiently unfearful of each other to seldom trouble to lock their doors' (p.17). The Clutter murders therefore spark an crisis of faith for the community – people feel alienated and disoriented, as though they have been 'told there is no God'. The ephemerality of life, and of the American dream, is starkly highlighted by the Clutter murders, and the subsequent auction of all the worldly goods they had striven to acquire. Furthermore, people are for the first time enduring 'the unique experience of distrusting each other' (p.96). The community's desire for the case to be solved underscores a psychological need to be able to return to their previous state of naivety, a desire that Capote's fictionalised ending suggests is largely achieved.

Key point

It is clear that, like the other members of the community in which they lived, the Clutters never conceived of the possibility of their murders. They did nothing to resist Dick and Perry, believing that, if they complied with the men's wishes, they would be safe.

The role of faith in society

Key quotes

'[I]n Finney County one is still within the Bible Belt borders, and therefore a person's church affiliation is the most important factor influencing his class status.' (p.45)

'Genesis Nine, Verse Six: "Whoso sheddeth man's blood, by man shall his blood be shed."' (Logan Green, p.304)

It is emphasised from the beginning of *In Cold Blood* that Finney County (of which Holcomb is a part) places great importance on Christian values and faith, with a 'combination of Baptists, Methodists and Roman Catholics' accounting for 'eighty per cent of the county's devout' and the rest, the 'élite', being 'Presbyterians and Episcopalians' (p.45). The church is central to the social life of the town, and faith is seen as a necessary attribute to achieve one's dreams 'with the help of God' (p.87). Yet church affiliation is also revealed to be 'the most important factor influencing [a person's] class status' (p.45) and Capote suggests that 'trust in God' (p.39) provides little protection from the outcasts of society, whose lack of faith means that immoral actions are not inhibited. Capote accedes that Christian faith can motivate individuals like Mrs Meier and Don Cullivan to extend the hand of friendship to those less fortunate than them, 'the salvation of a soul' (p.288) their primary purpose. However, he also suggests that Christianity can be used to justify cruelty. The hypocrisy of some people of faith is exemplified by the nuns who cared for Perry in an orphanage, whom he describes as 'shrouded disciplinarians who whipped him for wetting his bed' (p.100), and by the prosecuting attorney Logan Green who uses outdated passages from the Old Testament to justify the death penalty to a jury of 'presumed' (p.303) Christians. Thus, Capote suggests that, while faith has the potential to be a redemptive force in peoples' lives, it can also be used as a tool of oppression that further marginalises those less fortunate.

Mental health and the justice system

Key quotes

'Confined as he was by the M'Naughten Rule ... Dr Jones was impotent.' (p.293)

'I didn't realize what I'd done till I heard the sound.' (Perry, p.247)

Although Dick and Perry's guilt is never in doubt, Capote conspicuously brings into question the justice of the criminal proceedings brought against them. Throughout the text, significant space is devoted to consideration of Perry's traumatic past, thus establishing him as a tragic hero whose difficult experiences contributed to the development of his criminal psychopathology. This extensive exploration and compassionate treatment of Perry's character can be interpreted as an attempt by Capote to exonerate, or at least to some extent excuse, Perry. This interpretation is reinforced by the detailed narrative of the court proceedings. Capote reveals that Dr Jones is prevented from putting forward his complex psychiatric analyses of Dick and Perry because of the M'Naughten Rule. The M'Naughten Rule, described by Capote as 'a formula quite colour-blind to any permutations between black and white' forces Dr Jones to answer with a simple 'yes or no' to the question of whether the defendants 'knew right from wrong at the time of the commission of the crime' (p.293). Dr Jones is thus prevented from providing his extensive consideration and diagnoses of the defendants, which the more lenient Durham Rule would have allowed.

In an invitation to his readers to become judges of the legal system itself, Capote includes Dr Jones' inadmissible findings on both Dick and Perry in the text. Dr Jones reveals that Dick shows 'signs of emotional abnormality' and states that 'organic brain damage ... cannot be completely ruled out' (p.294). He concludes that Dick 'shows fairly typical characteristics of what would psychiatrically be called a severe character disorder' (p.295). These revelations call into question the degree to which Dick is culpable for his actions. Perry's culpability is brought into even greater doubt. Dr Jones believes that Perry's 'ability to separate the real situation from his own mental projections is very poor' (p.297) and that his 'present personality structure is very nearly that of a paranoid schizophrenic reaction' (p.298). Dr Jones' conclusions are corroborated by Dr Joseph Satten of the Menninger Clinic, 'a widely respected veteran in the field of forensic psychiatry' (p.298). Dr Satten contends that 'only the first murder matters psychologically, and that when Smith attacked Mr Clutter he was under a mental eclipse, deep inside a schizophrenic darkness' (p.302), a conclusion that seems to fit with Perry's statements that, 'I didn't want to harm the man. I thought he was a very nice gentleman. Soft-spoken. I thought so right up to the moment I cut his throat' (p.246), and 'I didn't realize what I'd done till I heard the sound' (p.247). Capote's decision to present this information undermines the courtroom proceedings, suggesting that for the trial to be fair, the jury should have been privy to this expert testimony.

Key point

Parallels can be drawn between Perry and his fellow Death Row inmate Lowell Lee Andrews, who is found to have the 'primary illness of separation of thinking from feeling' (p.316) as a consequence of schizophrenia. Andrews' case, which is the basis for a failed attempt to challenge the M'Naughten Rule, would have allowed 'confinement in the State Hospital for the Criminally Insane' (p.316). The reader is left to contemplate whether this would have been a more appropriate and humane option for protecting the community from Perry than to hang him 'in cold blood'.

Capital punishment

Key quotes

> 'At the time not a soul in sleeping Holcomb heard them – four shotgun blasts that, all told, ended six human lives.' (p.17)
>
> 'Look at their eyes. I'll be damned if I'm the only killer in the courtroom.' (Perry, p.288)

Capote presents the reader with a stanza from the poem 'Ballade des pendus' by François Villon at the start of the text. In this poem, Villon is speaking to the spectators at a hanging, telling them that hatred for those who are hanging gains them nothing, and that forgiveness is a far better path. The inclusion of this poem foregrounds the issue of capital punishment, prompting the reader to consider what is gained by taking a life for a life. The issue is also cleverly introduced in the title of the text itself, for while the 'cold blood' initially seems to refer to the Clutter murders, it can also be understood to refer to the 'judicial homicide' (p.325) of capital punishment.

Throughout the text, and particularly in Part 4, it is clear that the people of Kansas need to reinstate a sense of normality in their lives. Capote implies that this can only be achieved through the death penalty because 'in Kansas there is no such thing as life imprisonment without possibility of parole' (p.258). The state cannot risk Dick and Perry being released back into the community and therefore does everything possible to ensure the death penalty is given. During the *voir dire* examination of potential jurors for the trial, the reader is informed that many potential jurors 'won dismissal ... because they opposed capital punishment', while the impartiality of selected jurors is brought into question by the revelation that one juror stated of capital punishment: 'Ordinarily I'm against it. But in this case, no' (p.273). When prosecuting attorney Green argues that 'if ever there was a case in which the maximum penalty was justified, this is it' (p.304), he speaks for the majority of Kansans, though a few consider the action of hanging a man to be 'pretty goddam cold-blooded too' (p.306). Capote encourages the reader to consider whether capital punishment is really the most appropriate sanction, particularly given the weight of the testimony of the psychiatrists which, while not presented at trial, is laid out in detail in *In Cold Blood*.

Capote not only suggests that capital punishment is nothing more than sacrificial violence against the *'poor and friendless'* (p.258) but that it is in itself a cruel practice. He graphically describes the hanging of several criminals, noting that the state doctor at Andrews' hanging weeps at his duty, as Andrews' 'heart kept beating for nineteen minutes' (p.332). Similarly, at Dick's hanging it is 'a full twenty minutes' (p.339) before he is pronounced dead, and the dialogue between a reporter and a guard reveals that Dick could be heard 'gasping for breath' (p.340). Finally, at Perry's execution, Capote uses Dewey's character to express discomfort over the hanging despite his belief that 'capital punishment is a deterrent to violent crime', for the sight of Perry's 'childish feet, tilted, dangling' fails to give him the 'sense of climax, release, of a design justly completed' that he had expected (p.341).

Key point

In an interview with journalist George Plimpton in 1966, Capote stated: 'I feel that capital crimes should all be handled by Federal Courts, and that those convicted should be imprisoned in a special Federal prison where, conceivably, a life sentence could mean, as it does not in state courts, just that.'

Nature versus nurture

Key quotes

'[W]ho had ever given a damn about him?' (Perry, p.56)

'[A] small-time chiseller who got out of his depth, empty and worthless' (Alvin Dewey about Dick Hickock, p.341)

In Cold Blood contemplates whether an individual's nature is the primary force in shaping them into a criminal, or whether the environment in which they are raised is a more significant factor. Dr Jones' testimony raises the possibility that Dick suffers from a 'severe character disorder' (p.295) as a consequence of his car accident years earlier, but Capote's portrayal of Dick suggests that he was naturally oriented towards a life of crime and that his criminality was born, at least in part, from a desire to be 'normal' through the acquisition of wealth. This predilection towards such amoral behaviour that he would 'steal the weights off a dead man's eyes' is pointedly presented as a result of some flaw within Dick's own nature rather than a consequence of his upbringing by 'plain, honest people' (p.171).

In contrast, the portrayal of Perry provokes the reader to consider that he was not a natural-born killer, and that perhaps his actions resulted from an unhappy childhood. Long texts written by Perry's sister, his father, Dr Jones, and Willie-Jay create a composite image of Perry as a 'savable' (p.53) man of talent and sensitivity whose mind was warped by neglect, abuse and trauma at the hands of multiple authority figures. Capote's characterisation of Perry suggests that, if Perry had been given the love and kindness he needed, rather than growing up 'without direction, without love, and without ever having absorbed any fixed sense of moral values' (p.296), his life might have turned out very differently. Capote's criticism is aimed not only at Perry's family, but also at institutions like the orphanage that enhanced Perry's homicidal potential by traumatising him rather than caring for him.

Key point

The crime scene in the Clutter home reveals Perry's latent sensitivity, for amid the violence of the deaths are indications of compassion, such as the pillow under Kenyon's head. These touches reveal Perry's capacity for empathy, which was warped by years of abuse and neglect.

Fate versus free will

Key quotes

'The compulsively superstitious person is also very often a serious believer in fate; that was the case with Perry.' (p.53)

'You are a human being with a *free will*.' (Barbara Johnson to Perry, p.149)

To what extent do an individual's own actions determine what happens to them? To what extent do factors beyond an individual's control shape their lives? These questions are central to Capote's exploration of the themes of fate and free will in *In Cold Blood.*

There are multiple moments in the text in which small twists of fate appear to significantly influence the course of the characters' lives. Perry initially returns to Kansas in the hope of being reunited with Willie-Jay, believing the 'the journey's aftermath was up to fate' and that if things do not 'work out with Willie-Jay' then he will 'consider Dick's proposition'. It appears that if Perry had not missed Willie-Jay by 'only five hours' (p.56), then he would never have entered the Clutter home with Dick. It could also be argued that, had Dick purchased black stockings from the nuns as Perry wanted, their ability to conceal their identities would have nullified the need to kill the Clutters.

Fate (or luck) also appears to play a role in other key moments of the text. Floyd Wells pointedly remarks that if he had never met Dick, then 'maybe Mr Clutter wouldn't be in his grave' (p.163) and Alvin Dewey laments that the discovery of the identity of the murders 'just seems like a piece of luck' though he is certain that he would have 'hit this Wells' (p.167) in the course of his investigations. In addition, it is sheer coincidence that Perry has collected his box of belongings containing the incriminating boots just moments before his arrest.

However, Capote encourages the reader to consider the role of free will in Dick and Perry's actions as well. After the murders, Dick and Perry discuss Perry's belief in 'that premonition stuff' (p.99) and Dick asks a highly pertinent question: 'If you were so damn sure you were gonna crack up, why didn't you call it quits?' (p.99). Perry abdicates responsibility for his own actions when he responds that 'once a thing is set to happen, all you can do is hope it won't' (p.100). His desire to blame his actions on forces outside his control is central to his sister Barbara's criticisms of him. Her forceful assertion that 'what you have done, whether *right* or *wrong,* is *your own doing'* (p.147) reminds the reader that human beings have free will, and thus directs attention to the many opportunities Perry had to alter the course of events, such as the moment prior to the Clutter murders when he went outside and thought 'Why don't I walk off?' (p.243).

Key point

Like the people of Holcomb, Capote tries to make sense of the Clutter murders. His extensive consideration of the backgrounds of Dick and Perry, and of Perry's scarred psyche in particular, suggests that it is more than just fate that leads to the tragic series of events that culminates in the deaths of six people. However, he does imply that Perry's belief in fate plays a role in determining his actions on multiple occasions.

Sexuality

Though not a central element of the narrative, the sexual desires of Dick and Perry are established as relevant to understanding their natures and their psychopathology.

Sexual deviance

Key quotes

'He was sorry he felt as he did about her, for his sexual interest in female children was a failing of which he was "sincerely ashamed".' (p.204)

'[Perry] had "no respect for people who can't control themselves sexually".' (p.204)

In accordance with his repeated assertion that he is 'a normal' (p.204), Dick is often represented, particularly from Perry's point of view, as aggressively heterosexual and 'totally masculine' (p.28). As a man twice married and twice divorced, Dick seems incapable of fulfilling his sexual desires, conducting at least two relationships with women while in Mexico that are intense enough for the women to believe themselves engaged to him. Yet underlying Dick's masculine bravado there is a suggestion of deep-seated insecurities. These are first hinted at when he makes love to 'the younger of his betrotheds' (p.131), Inez, in a hotel room in Mexico, and whispers incessantly to her, 'Is it good baby? Is it good?' (p.153). Capote implies that Dick is constantly in need of affirmation of his masculinity in order to counter his shame at his 'sexual interest in female children'. Dick tries to justify his feelings, asserting that 'most real men had the same desires he had' (p.204), but his wish to keep these feelings secret is evidence that he knows his desires do not conform to societal expectations. It is revealed that Dick's motivation in going to the Clutter household had much to do with a desire to rape Nancy, an action Perry actively sought to prevent. Capote suggests that behind most criminal acts lies a desire that has not been satisfactorily met, a need that the criminal seeks to satisfy through the crime itself.

Key point

The revelation of Dick's sexual deviance reinforces his status as an abnormal outsider, further eroding any compassion the reader might feel for Dick while establishing Perry as the more 'normal' of the pair. This makes the later revelations in Part 3 of Perry's role in the killings even more astonishing for the reader.

Homosexual desire

Key quotes

'You are a man of extreme passion, a hungry man not quite sure where his appetite lies.' (Willie-Jay to Perry, p.54)

'Dick's literalness, his pragmatic approach to every subject, was the primary reason Perry had been attracted to him, for it made Dick seem, compared to himself, so authentically tough, invulnerable, "totally masculine".' (p.28)

Though Perry is never portrayed as homosexual, Capote imbues Perry's relationships with both Dick and Willie-Jay with homoerotic desire. In an interview with George Plimpton (1966), Capote said that Perry's 'love for Willie-Jay in the State Prison was profound – and it was reciprocated, but never consummated physically, though there was opportunity.' In his text Capote suggests that there is an intimate bond between the two men. That Perry may feel desire for Willie-Jay is suggested by the fact that Perry's 'portrait of Jesus' is endowed with 'Willie-Jay's full lips and grieving eyes' (p.54), and by Perry's repeated references to Willie-Jay as his 'real and only friend' (p.53). Willie-Jay becomes 'ten feet tall' in

Perry's memory, and his longing to be with the only man who had 'ever recognized his worth, his potentialities' is described as 'more alluring than any dream of buried gold' (p.56). It could be argued that, when Willie-Jay describes Perry as 'a hungry man not quite sure where his appetite lies' (p.54), the hunger he speaks of is a desire for a relationship with Willie-Jay. In 1950s America, homosexuals were considered a threat to the social order (the FBI kept a watch list of homosexuals, to monitor their activities); fulfilling such desires would have led to Perry, already an outsider and a social misfit, being further marginalised.

Perry's relationship with Dick might therefore be viewed as a reaction to his feelings for Willie-Jay. Perry's attraction to Dick is explained as an 'outgrowth of, and counterbalance to, the intensity of his admiration for the chaplain's clerk' (p.55). In contrast to Willie-Jay, Dick appears to conform to cultural expectations of masculinity – he is 'authentically tough' and 'totally masculine' (p.28) and, perhaps more importantly, he exhibits the homophobia typical of contemporary society when he scornfully says of Willie-Jay, '*He's* the faggot' (p.55). Yet Dick is clearly subjected to Perry's sexual gaze; as the two men clean themselves up in preparation for their journey to the Clutter home, Dick is described as 'an athlete constructed on a welterweight scale' (p.42) and, once ready, the men are referred to as 'two dudes setting off on a double date' (p.43). In this and other moments in the narrative, there is an intensity in the pair's interactions, wherein Dick seeks to prove his masculinity through exhibitions of heterosexual prowess, while Perry seeks to prove his masculinity by exhibiting a potential for violence.

A third relationship can also be considered to exist in the text – the unspoken relationship between Truman Capote and his subjects, and Perry in particular. This relationship is explored in the films *Infamous* and *Capote*.

Key point

It could be argued that Perry's desire to prove himself to Dick as equally masculine lies behind the violence of his actions in the Clutter household, and that the murders are therefore a result of his lack of fulfilment.

DIFFERENT INTERPRETATIONS

Different interpretations arise from different responses to a text. Over time, a text will evoke a wide range of responses from its readers, who may come from various social and cultural groups and live in very different places and historical periods. Responses by critics and reviewers can be published in in newspapers, journals and books, both online and in print. The can also be expressed in discussions among readers in the media, classrooms, book groups and so on.

While there is no single correct reading or interpretation of a text, it is important to understand that an interpretation is more than a personal opinion – it is the justification of a point of view on the text. To present an interpretation of a text based on your point of view, you must use a logical argument and support it with relevant evidence from the text.

Critical viewpoints

In Cold Blood has received both praise and criticism since it was first published in 1965. At the time of its publication, many heralded the nonfiction novel as a new and exciting work in which Capote was able to remain 'silent throughout the text and avoid influencing the trajectory of the events of the novel' (Leonard 2015). In 1966 George Steiner described *In Cold Blood* as 'a happening' that 'holds one spellbound' (Steiner 1965), while George Garrett, although concerned with the intrusion of narrative devices into the story, praised the 'literary excellency of the reporting job' (Garrett 1966). Subsequent positive reviews of Capote's work similarly praise the 'intricate process of poetic selection' (Almog 2012) that makes *In Cold Blood* deserving of being labelled 'literature'.

However, others have disagreed with this positive view of Capote's work, arguing that, perhaps as a consequence of his close personal relationship with the killers, Capote shaped the events in such a way that they misrepresent the truth and that the text is therefore not, as Capote claimed, a work of nonfiction. Stanley Kauffmann (1996) suggested that *In Cold Blood* did 'little more than recount a crime' and that Capote was 'the most outrageously overrated stylist of our time'. In contrast, Kenneth Tynan praised the quality of Capote's writing but asked whether what Capote did was 'morally defensible' (Almog 2012). Robert Siegle argues that an examination of Capote's narrative practice shows 'interpretive interests at work on the nonfiction material' (Siegle 1984) while Ralph Voss' recent extensive work on *In Cold Blood* argues that close study of the text brings into question Capote's claim that every word of the text was true. Various critics have been critical of Capote's research methodology, particularly his reliance on memory when taking notes, while others are critical of Capote's chosen narrative viewpoint, as, by writing himself out of the story, he distorts the truth of events.

Two interpretations of *In Cold Blood*

The following discussion shows how two contrasting interpretations of *In Cold Blood* can be equally plausible. Note that the two provide very different interpretations of the way in which form affects the presentation of ideas, issues and themes, but each is supported by evidence from the text, including references to characterisation, structure and plot.

Interpretation 1: Capote's use of the nonfiction novel form enhances the reader's understanding of the tragedy of the true events it depicts.

By dubbing *In Cold Blood* a 'nonfiction novel', Truman Capote made plain his intentions. Rather than simply reporting a series of events in the standard journalistic mode, he was imposing fictional techniques on rigorously collated documentary material. The creative decision to employ techniques such as narrative viewpoint, narrative structure and characterisation allows the author to give pattern and meaning to the Clutter murders, and thus shed light on the tragic nature of what occurred. Thus, while it cannot be denied that Capote has constructed a story, the essential truths of that story cannot be ignored.

The first important decision Capote made when he began writing *In Cold Blood* was to employ a heterodiegetic narrative voice (the voice of a narrator who does not take part in the plot), thus keeping himself separate from the events in the text. Although his involvement with the case, and particularly with the lives of the killers, is well documented, his presence within the narrative would disrupt the reader's capacity to behave as an alternative jury, weighing the evidence in order to understand what occurred. This is clear in the carefully reconstructed last movements of the Clutter family, such as when Nancy, in her final hours, lays out her clothes for church, including the 'dress in which she was to be buried' (p.67). Furthermore, Capote's refusal to take part in the plot, particularly in the trial of Dick and Perry, allows him to maintain a degree of independence from the material presented and thus enables readers to draw their own conclusions. In particular, readers can see that the Clutter family were the tragic victims of two psychologically scarred individuals.

Rather than simply being commented upon by the omniscient narrator, Dick and Perry's emotional and psychological scarring is revealed by Capote's masterful use of characterisation techniques. Capote brings his skills as a fiction writer to bear on his nonfiction subjects, cleverly characterising them by weaving thoughts with descriptions of physical appearance. Though Capote is often criticised for paying greater attention to the characterisation of Perry, he provides sufficient information about Dick for the reader to understand that it is his 'sexual interest in female children' (p.204) that draws him to the Clutter household. But it cannot be ignored that it is Perry who cuts Herb Clutter's throat and sets in motion the other killings. To understand what brought him to the point where his psychopathic rage manifests in violent murder, the reader must understand Perry's fantasy world and his traumatic background. His scarred nature is exemplified by his recurrent dream of the 'yellow bird' that functions as an 'avenging angel who savaged' (p.266) the various abusers at whose hands he had suffered over the years. It is only by fleshing out Perry's character in detail that the reader can understand his actions. Perry does indeed become an object of pity, but Capote does not exculpate him – he simply shows that the killer was a flawed and damaged individual.

The events of the murder are also given order through Capote's chosen narrative structure. In Part 1 of *In Cold Blood,* Capote develops two distinct but interwoven narrative threads that contrast the Clutter family's world with the world of their killers. The interpolation of the stories of the killers into that of the Clutters lends a tone of inevitability to the section, highlighting the tragedy of the lives cut short, particularly that of Nancy. Furthermore, throughout the text, Capote incorporates the voices of witnesses and fragments of documents to make the horrendous murder more 'real' and immediate. For example, Susan Kidwell's emphatic claim that Nancy has only suffered 'a nosebleed' reveals the shock experienced by those who witnessed the brutal consequences of the crime, and the reader shares in these feelings of dismay and disbelief when Nancy Ewalt declares that 'there's too much blood' (p.71). This further encourages readers to act in a manner analogous to jurors, as they are forced to bear witness to the realities of the world they live in, realities that cannot be ignored because this is a 'true account'.

Overall, Capote's use of the nonfiction novel form allows him to handle a large number of characters whose lives and fortunes are intricately and subtly interrelated, and thus provide a compelling exposition of a range of key themes and ideas. Capote successfully highlights the utter banality of the motivations for the Clutter murders and reveals confronting truths about a society whose refusal to accept responsibility for its damaged outcasts is at least in part responsible for the tragic loss that results from 'four shotgun blasts that, all told, ended six human lives' (p.17).

Interpretation 2: Capote's use of the nonfiction novel form presents a highly personal view of events and people, despite the appearance of objectivity.

As Capote himself admitted in an interview with George Plimpton (1966), 'in the nonfiction novel one can ... manipulate'. An examination of the techniques he employs in *In Cold Blood* reveals the truth of this statement. Despite the appearance of objectivity, by exerting his creative control over the information presented to his readers, Capote develops a narrative that allows him to convey a highly subjective view of people and events.

The appearance of objectivity in *In Cold Blood* is enhanced by Capote's use of an omniscient narrator who remains, for the most part, removed from the events of the text. As a consequence, it is easy for the reader to overlook the fact that every piece of information that Capote incorporates into the narrative has been collected, edited and carefully placed, in order to support his narrative purpose. There is no mention of the presence of the author or of his fact-finding process within the text, yet careful scrutiny reveals the way in which the narrator's subtle judgements guide the reader's responses. For example, the narrator's observations regarding Alvin Dewey's professionalism and determination position Dewey as the hero of the narrative, while the inclusion of multiple incidents demonstrating Dick's callousness – such as his running over dogs and his predatory behaviour towards the young girl on the beach – encourage the reader to reject him.

The highly personal nature of Capote's narrative is heightened by his inclusion of the reactions of various individuals involved in the case. These comments were made to Capote in the course of his investigative process in the months and years following the murders. The individuals who made them were burdened by the grief and trauma of the recent horrific events. Thus, Herb Clutter is remembered as 'a gentleman' (p.47) while Nancy is remembered for her 'kindliness' (p.31); hardly a negative word about the Clutter family is heard. Including these emotional and sympathetic perspectives on events enhances the tragedy for the reader, who is positioned to keenly feel the loss of the Clutter family in a similar way to the townspeople.

Capote's representation of Perry Smith most clearly reveals the power of the nonfiction novel to shape ostensibly objective factual material into an intimate portrayal of a character intended to evoke the reader's sympathy. It is well documented that Capote and Smith shared a bond forged by their common experiences of familial neglect and rejection. When Capote looked at Smith, he saw 'his shadow, his dark side, the embodiment of his own accumulated angers and hurts' (Clarke 1988), and this recognition elicited a degree of compassion for the murderer, which is detectable in the narrative. This compassion is most evident in Capote's intentional incorporation of various fictional scenarios. As De Bellis (1979) has revealed, Mrs Josie Meier denied Capote's claim in the text that Smith cried and said, 'I'm embraced by shame' when he was sentenced to death, while various witnesses at the execution of Smith vehemently refute the last words attributed to him before he was hanged. This blending of fiction and nonfiction elements – reflected in the categorisation of the text as a 'nonfiction novel' – enable Capote to partially redeem Smith by complicating his characterisation. Rather than depicting him simply as a cruel and one-dimensional character, Capote instead suggests that he is a pitiable figure.

Ultimately, while the nonfiction novel form gives the appearance of objectivity, the novelistic features employed by Capote amplify readers' emotional engagement with characters and events. The subjective process of selecting evidence and creating characters, hidden by the omniscient narrative viewpoint, prompts feelings such as fear and pity as readers feel that they too have come to know the individuals caught up in these tragic events.

QUESTIONS & ANSWERS

This section focuses on your analytical writing on the text, and gives you strategies for producing high-quality responses in your coursework and exam essays.

Essay writing – an overview

An essay on a literary text is a formal and serious piece of writing that presents your point of view on the text, usually in response to a given essay topic. Your 'point of view' in an essay is your interpretation of the meaning of the text's language, structure, characters, situations and events, supported by detailed analysis of textual evidence.

Analyse – don't summarise

In your essays it is important to avoid simply summarising what happens in a text.

- A **summary** is a description or paraphrase (retelling in different words) of the characters and events. For example: 'Macbeth has a horrifying vision of a dagger dripping with blood before he does to murder King Duncan.'
- An **analysis** is an explanation of the real meaning or significance that lies 'beneath' the text's words (and images, for a film). For example: 'Macbeth's vision of a bloody dagger shows how deeply uneasy he is about the violent act he is contemplating, and conveys his sense that supernatural forces are impelling him to act.'

A limited amount of summary is sometimes necessary to let your reader know which part of the text you wish to discuss. However, always keep this to a minimum and follow it immediately with your analysis of what this part of the text is really telling us.

Plan your essay

Carefully plan your essay so that you have a clear idea of what you are going to say. The plan ensures that your ideas flow logically, that your argument remains consistent and that you stay on the same topic. An essay plan should be a list of **brief dot points** – no more than half a page.

Include your central argument or main contention – a concise statement (usually in a single sentence) of your overall response to the topic. See 'Analysing a Sample Topic' for guidelines on how to formulate a main contention.

Write three or four dot points for each paragraph, indicating the main idea and evidence/examples from the text. Note that in your essay you will need to *expand* on these points and *analyse* the evidence.

Structure your essay

An essay is a complete, self-contained piece of writing. It has a clear beginning (the introduction), middle (several body paragraphs) and end (the last paragraph or conclusion). It must also have a central argument that runs throughout, linking each paragraph to form a coherent whole. See examples of introduction and conclusions in the 'Analysing a Sample Topic' and 'Sample Answer' sections.

The introduction establishes your overall response to the topic. It includes your main contention and outlines the main evidence you will refer to in the course of the essay. Write your introduction *after* you have done a plan and *before* you write the rest of the essay.

The body paragraphs argue your case – they present evidence from the text and explain how this evidence supports your argument. Each body paragraph needs:

- **a strong topic sentence** (usually the first sentence) that states the main point behind made in the paragraph.
- **evidence** from the text, including some brief quotations.
- **analysis** of the textual evidence, with explanation of its significance and how it supports your argument.
- **links back to the topic** in one or more statements, usually towards the end of the paragraph.

Connect the body paragraphs so that your discussion flows smoothly. Use some linking words and phrases such as 'similarly' and 'on the other hand', though don't start every paragraph like this. Another strategy is to use a significant word from the last sentence of one paragraph in the first sentence of the next.

Use key terms from the topic – or synonyms for them – throughout, so the relevance of your discussion to the topic is always clear.

The conclusion ties everything together and finishes the essay. It includes strong statements that emphasise your central argument and provide a clear response to the topic.

Avoid simply restating the points made earlier in the essay – this will end on a very flat note and imply that you have run out of ideas and vocabulary. The conclusion should be a logical extension of what you have written, not just a repetition or summary of it. Writing an effective conclusion can be a challenge. Try using these tips:

- Start by linking back to the final sentence of the second-last paragraph – this helps your writing to flow, rather than leaping back to your main contention straight away.
- Use synonyms and expressions with equivalent meanings, to vary your vocabulary. This allows you to reinforce your line of argument without being repetitive.
- When planning your essay, think of one or two broad statements or observations about the text's wider meaning. These should be related to the topic and your overall argument. Keep them for the conclusion, since they will give you something 'new' to say but still follow logically from your discussion. The introduction will be focused on the topic, but the conclusion can present a wider view of the text.

Essay topics

1. 'Truman Capote's *In Cold Blood* suggests that family relationships shape our identity.' Discuss.
2. In what way could it be argued that a desire for salvation lies behind the actions of the major characters in *In Cold Blood?*
3. 'The ability to live a normal life within the boundaries of acceptable society determines the likelihood of achieving one's dreams.'
   To what extent is this true for the characters in *In Cold Blood?*
4. "It can't be, there must be some mistake, things like that don't *happen*."
   What impact do the Clutter murders have on the community of Holcomb?
5. '*In Cold Blood* demonstrates the hypocrisy and the inhumanity of the American criminal justice system.' Discuss.
6. Is *In Cold Blood* truly a nonfiction novel as Truman Capote claimed, or is it better categorised as fiction?
7. How does Capote manipulate the reader in order to support the purpose of his book?
8. Consider the multiple meanings intended by Capote when he titled his work *In Cold Blood*.
9. 'Dick and Perry's criminal tendencies are a consequence of a lack of fulfilment.'
   Do you agree?
10. 'The capacity for religion to be either a restrictive or a redemptive force is revealed in the lives of Capote's characters.' Discuss.

Analysing a sample topic

"It can't be, there must be some mistake, things like that don't happen." What impact do the Clutter murders have on the community of Holcomb?

When presented with a topic that includes a quote from the text, ensure you consider the importance of both the quote and the question or direction. The quote component of the topic above, said by Mrs Bob Johnson, is a clear expression of an inability to comprehend what has happened. The key word in the question – 'impact' – should be used to frame your ideas. Thus, your essay could consider the way different members of the community respond to the news of the murder. It could also consider the impact of the killings in the longer term.

Sample introduction

> In the close community of Holcomb, a place where 'drama' never occurs, the murders of four members of the Clutter family sent shockwaves through the community. Truman Capote set out to write a nonfiction novel documenting the responses of this community. In the course of his research, Capote discovered that the people of Holcomb were experiencing an epistemological crisis, as they could not understand how anyone could want to destroy such an upstanding family. This crisis sparks feelings of fear and mistrust of one another, feelings that can only be healed by reinstating a sense of normalcy through whatever means necessary.

Body paragraph outline

Paragraph 1: Most members of the Holcomb community struggle to find an explanation for why anyone would murder the Clutter family.

- Herb was a 'man's man' and a 'die-hard community booster' who was 'known for his equanimity, his charitableness'. Nancy was 'pretty and popular'.
- The deaths were unimaginable: 'I can't imagine you afraid. No matter what happened, you'd talk your way out of it' (Mrs Ashida).
- Denial was a common response: 'It's only a nosebleed' (Susan Kidwell); 'You had to believe it, because it was really true' (Larry Hendricks); 'But who hated the Clutters?' (Mrs Hartman); 'How was it possible that such effort, such plain virtue, could overnight be reduced to this – smoke?' (Andy Erhart).

Paragraph 2: Following the initial shock of the murders, feelings of fear and mistrust manifest. The townspeople feed one another's reactions to the crimes.

- Before the murders, nobody used to lock doors; shock becomes suspicion and fear.
- 'If it wasn't [the man in the airplane], maybe it was you. Or somebody across the street. All the neighbours are rattlesnakes' (Myrtle Clare).
- The typical response was 'amazement, shading into dismay; a shallow horror sensation that cold springs of personal fear swiftly deepened.'
- 'Now we don't know what to think. It must have been a grudge killing. Done by somebody who knew the house inside out' (Mrs Hartman).
- 'Of what were they frightened? "It might happen again."'

Paragraph 3: A desire for retribution and a return to normalcy marked the feelings of the community following the arrest of the murderers.

- 'We can't go on like this. Distrusting everybody, scaring each other to death' (Mrs Hartman).
- 'Ask me, we've had enough excitement' (Myrtle Clare).
- 'They're not going to hurt anybody ever again' (Alvin Dewey).
- 'I hope they keep 'em locked up good. I won't feel easy knowing they're in our vicinity' (Mrs Hartman).
- Logan Green appeals to the jurors' fear when he warns 'the next time they go slaughtering it may be *your* family.'

Paragraph 4: Having achieved retribution, people seem able to move on with their lives.

- Capote's fictionalised ending, in which Dewey encounters Susan Kidwell, suggests that, with the killers locked up, the townspeople have been able to move on.
- 'Deaths, births, marriages – why just the other day he'd heard that Nancy Clutter's boy friend, young Bobby Rupp, had gone and got married' (Dewey).

Sample conclusion

> From Capote's closing scene, it seems that although the murders of the Clutter family created both despair and dismay in the days following the tragic event, these feelings were not to last forever. The capacity for the community of Holcomb to exact retribution on the killers by removing them from their physical world enabled them to return to their everyday lives. Thus, it appears that the Clutter killings had little long-term impact on their community, and memories of the Clutter family scattered like their belongings, then became whispers of 'wind voices in the wind-bent wheat'.

SAMPLE ANSWER

'Dick and Perry's criminal tendencies are a consequence of a lack of fulfilment.' Do you agree?

Perhaps the most startling image to emerge from Truman Capote's nonfiction novel *In Cold Blood* is that of the sad and brutal America in which Dick and Perry have grown up. For both men, life has been a series of disappointments and setbacks that have led them to pursue a life of crime in order to fulfil their desire for economic independence. However, it is not only a petty desire for money that lies behind the men's criminality; Perry is burdened by psychological scars from his traumatic childhood that leave him with a desire for vengeance against those who have hurt him, while Dick wishes to satisfy his sexual predilections.

From the biographical accounts given of Dick, it is clear to the reader that he had little opportunity for economic mobility in his life. Dick's honest and hardworking parents make it clear that they 'never have had any money', so, rather than accepting one of the 'offers from two colleges to play ball', when Dick left school he instead went to work on the Santa Fe railroad. In his efforts to fulfil his desire to live a life that conformed to the notion of the American dream, he 'was in debt all the time' and so fell into the habit of passing bad cheques. It is clear that, at the age of twenty-eight, Dick continues to feel a sense of frustration at his inability to achieve economic success. Capote makes this frustration obvious through the personification of 'Envy', which is said to be 'constantly with him' and is directed at anyone who 'had anything he wanted to have'. Ironically, such feelings prompt Dick to pursue a life of crime so that he might live 'a regular life'. However, the pursuit of wealth is not the only cause underlying Dick's criminal tendencies.

A far darker need fuelling his criminal actions is a desire to satisfy his sexual urges. Dick is characterised by Capote as 'totally masculine', but his masculinity is revealed to be toxic and perverted. Though he seeks to keep his 'sexual interest in female children' a secret, it is a source of shame that contradicts his repeated claim to be 'a normal'. Dick's paedophilic tendencies are first revealed when he seeks to seduce the young girl on the beach, but are most fully realised in his written autobiography for Dr Jones. In this document, Dick confesses that his principal motivation in going to the Clutter house was 'not to rob them but to rape the girl'. He also chillingly alludes to 'other things' that he is too ashamed to admit, 'afraid of [his] people finding them out'. These desires appear central to Dick's inability to control his criminal impulses, and suggest that he seeks to satiate his desires through crime even though, as he himself claims, 'I know it is wrong'.

Although poverty is a barrier to success for Perry, his tendency towards violence seems to stem less from pecuniary concerns than from an unconscious need to exact vengeance for his sufferings. The various pieces of documentary evidence, from those who have known Perry, that Capote includes in his text present a composite image of a man of talent and sensitivity whose parents' neglect meant that he grew up 'without direction, without love'. This neglect, coupled with multiple episodes of abuse at the hands of 'authority figures' leave Perry psychologically scarred and prone to 'violent assaultive behaviour' that occurs in a 'schizophrenic darkness'. Perry's need for vengeance, made clear by his recurrent dream of a 'yellow bird' that functions as an 'avenging angel who savaged his enemies', appears to be the cause of his violence towards Herb Clutter. This is corroborated by Perry's claim that, 'I didn't realize what I'd done' until after he had cut Herb's throat. Perry's violent actions suggest that the absence of love in his life, or even a sufficiently fulfilling friendship, such as that which Willie-Jay might have provided, left a gaping psychological wound that prompts his outbursts.

Though the immorality of Dick and Perry's criminal actions is unquestionable, Capote's account suggests that, for some people at least, criminality emerges from an intense desire to compensate for or address a need in the individual's life. Although it appears that both men's conscious reason for going to the Clutter house was to acquire wealth to address their financial needs, unconsciously both Dick and Perry ultimately perform their most horrific crimes in order to fulfil deeper desires. Dick's paedophilic urges and Perry's desire for vengeance propel them on a destructive path that leads to the tragic deaths of four members of the Clutter family.

REFERENCES & READING

Text

Capote, T 1965, *In Cold Blood*, Penguin, Melbourne.

References

Books and journal articles

Almog, S 2012, 'Representations of Law and the Nonfiction Novel: Capote's *In Cold Blood* Revisited', *International Journal for the Semiotics of Law*, vol.25, pp.355–68.

Clarke, G 1988, *Truman Capote: A Biography*, Carroll & Graf, New York.

Conniff, B 1993 '"Psychological Accidents": *In Cold Blood* and Ritual Sacrifice', *Midwest Quarterly*, vol.35, no.1, pp.77–93.

Connolly, O & Haydar, B 2008, 'The Case Against Faction', *Philosophy and Literature*, vol.32, no.2, pp.347–58

De Bellis, J 1979, 'Visions and Revisions: Truman Capote's *In Cold Blood*', *Journal of Modern Literature*, vol.7, no.3, pp.519–36

Garrett, G 1966, 'Crime and punishment in Kansas: Truman Capote's *In Cold Blood*', in *Hollins Critic*, vol.3, no.1, p.1.

Hollowell, J 1997 "Capote's *In Cold Blood*: The Search for Meaningful Design," *Arizona Quarterly*, vol.53, no.3, pp. 97–115.

Kim, L 2001, 'Critical Essay on *In Cold Blood*', *Nonfiction Classics for Students Presenting Analysis, Context, and Criticism on Nonfiction Works*. Eds D Galens, J Smith and E Thomason, vol.2, Gale, Detroit.

Leonard, S 2015, 'Journalism as Artistic Expression: The Critical Response to Truman Capote's *In Cold Blood*', *Tulane Undergraduate Research Journal*, vol.2, pp.6–12.

Madison Davis, J 2012, 'Recognizing the Art of Nonfiction: Literary Excellence in True Crime', *World Literature Today*, September/October, pp.10–12.

Siegle, R 1984, 'Capote's "Handcarved Coffins" and the Nonfiction Novel', *Contemporary Literature*, vol.25, no.4, pp.437–51.

Skalevag, S 2012, 'Truth, Law and Forensic Psychiatry in Truman Capote's *In Cold Blood*', *Law and Humanities*, vol.6, no.2, pp.243–59.

Voss, R 2011, *Truman Capote and the Legacy of* In Cold Blood, The University of Alabama Press, Alabama.

Wood, M 1988, 'Immortality at any price', *The Times Literary Supplement*, Issue 4457, p.950.

Newspaper and magazine articles

Capote, T 1965, 'In Cold Blood', *The New Yorker*, 25 September.

Garden City Telegram 1959, 'Clutter Family Slayings Shock, Mystify Area', 16 December, p.1.

Kauffman, S 1966, 'Capote in Kansas', *New Republic*, 23 January, https://newrepublic.com/article/114887/stanley-kauffmann-truman-capotes-cold-blood

Plimpton, G 1966, 'The Story Behind a Nonfiction Novel', *The New York Times*, 16 January, http://www.nytimes.com/books/97/12/28/home/capote-interview.html

Steiner, G 1965, 'A cold-blooded happening: "In Cold Blood" by Truman Capote', *The Guardian*, 2 December.

Film and television

Capote 2005, dir. Bennett Miller, Sony Pictures. Starring Philip Seymour Hoffman, Clifton Collins Jr and Catherine Keener.

In Cold Blood 1967, dir. Richard Brooks, Columbia Pictures. Starring Robert Blake, Scott Wilson and John Forsythe.

In Cold Blood TV miniseries 1996, dir. Jonathan Kaplan. Starring Anthony Edwards, Eric Roberts and Sam Neill.

Infamous 2006, dir. Douglas McGrath, Warner Brothers. Starring Toby Jones, Daniel Craig and Sandra Bullock.

Websites

Fakazis, L, 'New Journalism' in *Encyclopaedia Britannica,* https://www.britannica.com/topic/New-Journalism

McMillan, N, 'Truman Capote' in *Encyclopedia of Alabama,* http://www.encyclopediaofalabama.org/article/h-1115.